NO MORE DRAMA

PROJECT PRESS / CARYSFORT PRESS

CONTENTS

INTRODUCTION: NO UNCERTAIN TERMS by Peter Crawley	P. 009
RIMINI PROTOKOLL: A LIVE ARCHIVE OF THE EVERYDAY by Christiane Kühl	P. 029
LOLA ARIAS: EXPANDING THE REAL by Cecilia Sosa	P. 046
THEATRE REMINDS ME OF POLITICS by Jacob Wren	P. 061
PHILIPPE QUESNE'S VIVARIUM STUDIO: A VIEWER'S VIEWS by Denise Luccioni	P. 081
MORE THAN A SYMPTOM: CURATING PERFORMING ARTS AS A JOB, CHALLENGE AND PURPOSE by Florian Malzacher	P. 099
POSITIVE ACTS: THE EVOLUTION OF PAN PAN THEATRE COMPANY by Noelia Ruiz	P. 119
DISJUNCTION AND THEATRICALITY: ELEVATOR REPAIR SERVICE'S GATZ AND NATURE THEATER OF OKLAHOMA'S NO DICE by Francisco Frazão	P. 141
GISÈLE VIENNE, THE STAGE OF DESIRE by Chantal Hurault	P. 163
WITHOUT GUILE: RICHARD MAXWELL AND THE NEW YORK CITY PLAYERS by Sarah Gorman	P. 177
CULTIVATED CHAOS: MOMENT SPECIFIC DRAMATURGY by Sodja Zupanc Lotker	P. 195
THE PEOPLE IN THE ROOM: A KIND OF CONVERSATION ABOUT QUARANTINE by Quarantine	P. 213

EDITED BY CRAWLEY & WHITE

NO UNCERTAIN TERMS   INTRODUCTION

PETER CRAWLEY

There comes a playful moment in Shakespeare's HAMLET when it seems that Polonius, prolix and tedious counsellor to the king, will list every form of theatre known to the world: "tragedy, comedy, history, pastoral, pastoral-comical, historical-pastoral, tragical-historical, tragical-comical-historical-pastoral; scene individable, or poem unlimited." To that litany, Ireland's Pan Pan Theatre Company recently added one more form during its radical version of Shakespeare's play when the actor Daniel Reardon eyeballed the audience, snapped out the term "postdramatic" and let a silence descend on the auditorium that seemed to last for an aeon.

Like much in that production, THE REHEARSAL, PLAYING THE DANE (2010) — which began with a brief academic lecture, involved three actors vying for the part of Hamlet (with the prince cast by audience vote), inserted a school production as "the play within the play" and still found ample room for sword fights, skulls, Elizabethan ruffs, Beckettian lifts and a memorable performance by a Great Dane — it was hard to know whether the reference was intended as giddy self send-up or an unblinking, solemn statement of intent. In the ambiguity of the moment, the audience giggled, fell silent, giggled again, fell silent again, and finally Reardon resumed his speech. Pan Pan's

Artistic Director, Gavin Quinn, has never laid explicit claim to postdramatic, although for twenty years the company has been making theatre like few others; a theatre in which text abounds but in which the play is not the thing.

It may seem strange to define the remit of NO MORE DRAMA in negative terms, but it is easier to say what the subject of our enquiry is not, than to settle on a single classification. The essays in this collection deal with contemporary forms of theatre which tend to resist rigid definition. Sometimes described as postdramatic theatre, documentary theatre or live art, this work does not begin with a writer or take a dramatic text as its basis. Rarely does it ask its performers to inhabit characters, or its audience to believe they are somewhere other than a performance space. Where once the theatre obeyed unities of time and space, of character and narrative, the art of the twentieth century moved from modernist atomisation to postmodern pluralism. Making meaning through fragmented experience, not the cohesive artefact of a play, this is theatre for which the centre could not hold.

The fleeting moments of all theatre makes it hard to contain, which is why the persistence of written text, the residue of the theatre event, tends

PETER CRAWLEY

to dominate critical reception and analysis. Yet the stubbornly ephemeral nature of performance has significance itself, ways of making meaning that deserve rigorous response. Here, then, is a concise but wide-ranging collection of company profiles, performance analysis, professional treatises and political provocations. Through fluid description, careful contextualising and punchy argument, we invite audiences, practitioners, students and anyone hungry to learn about the development of theatrical form to join an expanding conversation. It may not always be easy to categorise this style of theatre, but we know it when we see it.

NO BEEF

There will always be drama in theatre. Much as Hans-Thies Lehmann's descriptive text, *Postdramatic Theatre*,[1] understands "post" as a point of departure, not succession, so NO MORE DRAMA is not intended as a joyless imperative. If anything, the essays aim to demystify the methods of what is perhaps the latest chapter of the avant-garde, to edge towards an accessible language of appreciation, and, against an often hostile critical environment, or forbiddingly academic language, to introduce some cooling colloquialisms: Let's knock off the drama and can the theatrics. (We also like the Mary J. Blige song). The case of Germany's ground-breaking documentary theatre makers, Rimini Protokoll, was hardly unusual, whose earliest works were greeted by audiences and critics with equal parts enthusiasm and scepticism. Christiane Kühl begins her chapter on the company with a vivid illustration of the performance that put them on the map, DEUTSCHLAND 2 (2002), which recruited 666 citizens of the former German seat of power, Bonn, to occupy a disused plenary hall and relay, by earpiece, the speeches of 666 members of parliament streamed live from the Reichstag. Denounced as mockery by the President of the Bundestag, the performance was denied use of the Bonn space, and Kühl offers a trenchant interpretation: "the President apparently feared that politics may, in this context, be seen as that which it evidentially so often is: theatre." Instead, she argues (and as their title suggests), Rimini Protokoll were engaged in a sophisticated meditation on the problems of representation: if politicians are public representatives, how well do they represent the public and can the public also represent them?

So begins an exploration of the twenty-first century documentarians, who find their antecedents in the early twentieth century agit-prop montage of Erwin Piscator or the *teatro jornal* of Augusto Boal, but who place a new focus on bringing reality to the stage and audiences out into the world. Long distance truckers, Indian call centre-operators, Egyptian prayer callers, video game designers and company shareholders are as likely to inhabit their theatre. Non-professional performers all, their stories may ache with authenticity, yet they have been given no less consideration than anything else placed within a theatrical frame and the audience's interaction is crucial to Rimini Protokoll's dramaturgy: the experience communicates meaning. It is a theatre that may have lost its illusion, but not its capacity to illuminate.

NO BORDERS

All art is inescapably political, George Orwell maintained in his essay "Why I Write." "The opinion that art should have nothing to do with politics is itself a political attitude." Nor do the aesthetics of theatrical form, however seemingly discrete or disjointed, develop in a vacuum. In her essay on the theatre of Argentinean artist Lola Arias, "Expanding the Real," Cecilia Sosa sets the scene for a career that developed in a disintegrating city. Shortly after Arias debuted with LA ESCUÁLIDA FAMILIA, her grimly humourous depiction of a family dynamic so warped that even Eugene O'Neill might have called Social Services, the 2001 economic crisis of Argentina reached its flashpoint and Buenos Aires erupted in protests, riots and the fleeing of its President. Arias is not prophetic (for that, as Sosa points out, she has a soothsaying turtle) but her archly unsettling work is suffused with the restless anxieties of her time and place. "Arias's post-apocalyptic drama appears to insist that new social ties are needed in contemporary Argentina," writes Sosa, while characterising Arias and her peers as Argentina's "post-trauma" generation. "The distance that they have gained from loss allows them to see tragedy not only as an opportunity for pain, but also for humour and hope," writes Sosa of an artist reshaping her theatre, and, in so doing, reshaping her world.

Jacob Wren, co-artistic director of Montreal's PME-ART, may not seem quite as optimistic about the politics of form. A self-described (and self-effacing) "writer and maker of eccentric performances," Wren's provocation, "Theatre Reminds Me of Politics," addresses the cyclical nature of advances in artistic form and their inevitable co-option into the mainstream. "From my perspective, what happens, over and over, is that some new energy arises, a push towards different ways of making and thinking about theatre. This new energy, after being partially absorbed by the more traditional approach, is then substantially suppressed." Writing at a time when PME-ART faces its own crisis, uncertain as to whether it can continue to make work in Canada's current culture of funding cuts, Wren's analogy between the communities forged through political action and within auditoria draws from professional, personal and philosophical perspectives. At times cutting, often galvanising, it is always searching. "My analogy hinges on theatre and leftist politics sharing similar shades of idealism. The dream that things could be different."

NO TRADITION

Where do movements begin? When the critic Martin Esslin watched the elusive meaning, formal rupture and bleak humour shared by a group of playwrights in which "the certitudes and unshakable basic assumptions of former ages have been swept away" he called it *Theatre of the Absurd* and gave us new terms of reference to discuss Samuel Beckett, Eugene Ionesco, Harold Pinter, Günter Grass, Edward Albee and many others. Hans-Thies Lehmann did much the same thing when he observed shared concerns of method and manufacture among artists who no longer prioritised the dramatic text, such as Robert Wilson, Robert Lepage, Pina Bausch, the Wooster Group, Forced Entertainment, Theatre de Complicite, Socìetas Raffaello Sanzio and Gob Squad, cogently held together under the rubric of the postdramatic.

An artist like Philippe Quesne, for instance, does not break from the past just by concentrating on multimedia or by continually exposing the apparatus of theatrical illusion. He may, however, divert the course of the present. Promiscuous with its references and techniques, his first production with Vivarium Studios was widely scoffed at in France but more readily embraced abroad, as Denise Luccioni points out. But, with the Platonic allusions of its title, LA DÉMANGEAISON DES AILES (ITCHING OF WINGS, 2003) was more than a novelty and Quesne's work, reflecting reality through shifting shadows, might be the logical inheritor of Plato's allegory of the cave. "Vivarium Studio is about "doing," "acting," bonding, one of the main reasons for theatre to exist," Luccioni writes, as she brings Quesne's company ("proving to be terribly French but different from everything that is expected from the French") full circle: "Vivarium is going back further in time, before theatre, before ritual, back to getting out of the cave, merging visions and projections, back to the magic of coming out into the light."

NO REASON

In the coherence of a movement, or the making of a scene, the curator of performance plays a critical role. Whether these figures are festival programmers or the artistic directors of influential venues, they determine patterns in contemporary performance while reinforcing their aesthetics. Increasingly, though, these decisions have a global reach. One is as likely to see the work of Philippe Quesne in the Dublin Theatre Festival, Richard Maxwell's New York City Players at the KunstenfestivalDesArts in Brussels, or Pan Pan Theatre Company premiering its work at the Forum Freies Theater in Düsseldorf and the Shanghai Dramatic Arts Centre. Who are theatre's taste-makers? "Among the professions that are rather close to art or even right within it, but that are not artistic themselves—not directly artistic themselves—the curator has the youngest and most unclear profile," begins Florian Malzacher, curator and critic, as he reaches into art history, performance theory and the economics of the performance industry, to tease out a job description—one with substantial implications for the propagation and interpretation of theatrical form.

Ireland's Pan Pan Theatre Company clearly benefits from international courtship, an exposure that has fed its aesthetic from its first production, NEGATIVE ACT, in 1991, and which has made it arguably the foremost experimental theatre company within a culture more associated with the literary quality of its playwrights. In her profile of Pan Pan, Noelia Ruiz traces a convergence of influence—from the European avant-garde and the French "théâtre de boulevard" to idiosyncratic Futurist manifestos and the formal rigour of modernist design. She nods at symbolist drama and maps the intersection between postmodernism and postdramatic theatre, to end, somehow, with a stage on which MACBETH is reconceived as a school room lesson (MAC-BETH 7, 2004), Oedipus Rex mans a family barbecue as blood streams from his eye sockets over his shirt (OEDIPUS LOVES YOU, 2006), or the role of Hamlet is cast via democratic election. The performance text is often conspicuous in Pan Pan's work, albeit decentred, and Ruiz carefully traces the company's evolving aesthetic which never proscribes the dramatic canon.

PETER CRAWLEY

NO PLAY (AND ALL WORK)

Two American companies of the New York "downtown theatre" scene have recently chosen an unlikely setting for alternative performance: namely, the office space. In the drab, timeless room of Elevator Repair Service's GATZ (2006), an idle worker produces a copy of F. Scott Fitzgerald's *The Great Gatsby* and begins to read aloud while the fiction slowly permeates his space. From the cubicles of Nature Theatre of Oklahoma's production, NO DICE (2007), two office workers begin a conversation rooted in the banal exchanges of nine-to-five existence (its text was culled from 100 hours of phone conversations). "Both pieces dispel or challenge the demands of the dramatic," writes Francisco Frazão in his chapter, "Disjunction and Theatricality:" "Gatz through a refusal of adaptation, choosing to include the entire novel, verbatim, thus resisting the pared-down effectiveness of a play; NO DICE with a signal-to-noise ratio much lower than the naturalistic stylisation of dialogue. The two pieces, then, instead of doing without text altogether…interrogate its status in the context of performance." Taking a cue from the art critic Michael Fried, Frazão considers the nature of "absorption" in performance—the cast of GATZ are oblivious to the presence of an audience, whereas the "theatricality" of NO DICE's hammy office workers is an anxious response to the awareness they are being watched. Frazão considers the approach of both productions to time as both "an experience and a representation" (at seven and a half hours and four hours long, respectively, GATZ and NO DICE are unconventionally, self-consciously durational works) and pursues the meaning made through disjunction, where the rules of literature squares off with the conventions of performance and workers engage in a theatrical game whose rules are unknown to us. "Postdramatic theatre exposes the seamlessness between text and production for the ideological construct that it is," writes Frazão, "replacing coherence and cohesion with an aesthetics of mismatch." A similar gap between representation and the represented allows the electric charge of Gisèle Vienne's theatre, where dolls, puppets and masks enforce a disturbing disconnection between bodies and the force of life. Those spaces are filled with the chill of death and the surge of sexual desire, argues Chantal Hurault's "The Stage of Desire." "In the realms of art and erotism, dolls and mannequins are fetish objects, charged with a heavy history of contradictions, which, in their transgressive or immoral aspects, touch on religion as well as the marketplace. [...] We are at the heart of the contradiction between the forbidden and the transgression on which Georges Bataille bases his concept of erotism and Gisèle Vienne her work."

The work of Richard Maxwell and the affectless style of his New York City Players is controversial for quite different reasons, notes Sarah Gorman, pursuing a method that alienates those seeking emotive connection but beguiles those who find beauty in the quotidian and a hard-won aesthetic of "amateurishness". Gorman, who has followed Maxwell's theatre since 2001, finds an artist as sceptical of performative virtuosity as Rimini Protokoll or Pan Pan, but who resists any easy brackets. "I am regularly confounded by the new work I encounter," she admits; "just as I think I have a coherent overview of what he is about and how he experiments with theatrical form, he presents something which is a dramatic departure from what went before." Having read his work as a critique of individualism—a sustaining myth of American capitalism—the "hero" archetype in Maxwell's most recent work, **NEUTRAL HERO** (2011), seems to buck the trend again. Through persuasive reasoning, Gorman manages to locate the rupture within a larger march of Maxwell's work. "His characters are blue-collar workers, support staff, cowboys or working class citizens attempting to make sense of a rapidly changing environment. They try to reconcile their own inertia with the myth of freedom and equal opportunity promoted as part of The American Dream. Their inability to make sense of the contradictions they experience provides a vital counterpoint to the mainstream ideology of liberal capitalism promulgated internationally by the slick "professional" aesthetic of Hollywood films and TV exports."

NO CONNECTION

The playful chaos of postmodernism and the disjointed experience of much postdramatic theatre seem closely aligned. Today, contends Sodja Lotker, performances reflect a multiplicity of experiences in which the text is replaced by a discrete series of experiences; fragments offered to an audience in seemingly random configurations making the viewer responsible for the production's dramaturgy. Beginning with Árpád Schilling's renowned Krétakör, which in 2008, transformed from a Hungarian theatre ensemble into what we might call a loose collaboration of social choreographers, Lotker's essay, "Cultivated Chaos: Moment Specific Dramaturgy," proposes a new set of tools for theatrical composition and interpretation. "Total fragmentation," she writes, is the separation not only of scenes, ideas and themes but of the performance itself into different spaces, places, times, as well as a fragmentation of the audience…" With illustrations from the work of Gob Squad, Needcompany and others, Lotker is less interested in an anarchy of viewing, than how companies utilise chaos as units of composition—in "how much it makes sense" within our explosion of perspectives, the disorder of our times.

NO WORRIES

We conclude, fittingly, with Quarantine, the British company set up by directors Richard Gregory and Renny O'Shea and designer Simon Banham, who define themselves as a "shifting constellation of collaborators". Their collaboration with what Rimini Protokoll might call "everyday experts" is reflected in a piece composed by a group of their associates, who each respond to a series of questions about the company, the artform and its politics in an essay that reads partly like a philosophical enquiry, partly like a witty game. That may be the connecting thread of NO MORE DRAMA, and the theatre that engages us in surprising, revealing ways. "There's a camp that wants the grit, the conflict, the desire somehow made manifest onstage; engaged with or

PETER CRAWLEY

presented theatrically," considers Matt Fenton, director of Live at LICA. "And for them, work that doesn't do this, however well conceived or performed or structured, seems apolitical, or irrelevant; or at least just not theatre. For plenty of us though, a politics, and a sadness at why things are not, you know, different, is pretty clear in the work."

This enquiry into the state of the artform, an effort to tease out why people make the work they do, is to nourish the curious and to challenge the sceptics. As the poet writes:

> We just want y'all to have a good time
> No more drama in your life
> Work real hard to make a dime
> If you got beef — your problem, not mine.[2]

---

1. Lehmann, Hans-Thies *Postdramatic Theatre* trans. Jürs-Munby, Karen (London: Routledge, 2006)
2. Blige, Mary J. "Family Affair" from the album *No More Drama* (Universal Music, 2001)

RIMINI PROTOKOLL: A LIVE ARCHIVE OF THE EVERYDAY

CHRISTIANE KÜHL (TRANS. RACHEL WEST)

In Germany, in 2002, the hitherto largely unknown group, Rimini Protokoll, gained instant national attention with a project that almost did not take place at all. Two men who played a significant role in this were Matthias Lilienthal—who would become director of the Berlin theatre, Hebbel am Ufer, in the following year and make this venue the most important theatre for performing arts in the country—and Wolfgang Thierse, president of the German Bundestag. At that time Lilienthal was artistic director of the international theatre festival Theater der Welt. In this capacity he invited a loosely associated group of four young artists who had studied together and went by the name Rimini Protokoll to develop a project for the festival. As with all of their work, the artists let themselves be inspired by the place where the project should be shown. In this case, it was Bonn.

At that time, the post-war capital of the Federal Republic of Germany was going through a massive identity problem. For decades the city had been defined by the seat of government, but after the reunification, Berlin was chosen as the new/old German capital. After various ministries, the millennium saw the German Bundestag also making the move to Berlin; this despite the fact that a new plenary hall had recently been completed in Bonn at a cost of €120 million. The magnificent, translucent building by the architectural firm Behnisch and Partners, located directly on the Rhine, was now empty.

This void, this absence of politics, was the starting point for the project **DEUTSCHLAND 2 (GERMANY 2)**. The concept was as simple as it was surprising: On 27th June, 2002, a meeting of the German Bundestag in its new home, the Reichstag in Berlin, would be broadcast live to the recently vacated plenary hall in Bonn. Not via video screen and loudspeakers, but through individual earpieces, which would transmit the speech of each Berliner politician directly to the ears of the

A LIVE ARCHIVE OF THE EVERYDAY

same number of volunteer citizens in Bonn. In turn, these volunteers were given the task of relaying the words, much like a simultaneous translator, into the microphone at the lectern in Bonn. In the run-up to this kind of live re-enactment of *Realpolitik*, Rimini Protokoll sought, by means of newspaper advertisement, 666 citizens who were willing to represent the 666 German members of parliament on the 27th June, from 9am in the morning (Topic: Labour Market) until 2am at night (Topic: Wind Turbines). The original German word for "politician" is "Volksvertreter" which literally translates as "the person who stands in for the people." Rimini Protokoll wanted to explore what happens if the people stand in for the person who stands in for the people. If the people's representative is represented by the people.

The performance in the plenary hall never happened. The aforementioned Bundestag President, Wolfgang Thierse, stepped in personally and prohibited the use of the historical space, saying he felt "that the proposed procedure" would "impair the dignity and prestige of the German Bundestag." By doing this, the President basically misjudged his own people, because the video-casting for the participants alone had shown that most applicants had wanted to take part out of a genuine sense of identification, with the hope of speaking the words of one of their esteemed politicians. Unlike his citizens, the President apparently feared that politics may, in this context, be seen as that which it evidentially so often is: theatre. This prohibition by the President ultimately fuelled the entertainment value of the story, ensuring that DEUTSCHLAND 2 and the relationship between art and politics were discussed in all major national newspapers, including the news magazine Der Spiegel. In the end, the project took place in the auditorium of the Schauspielhalle Bonn Beuel, which Rimini Protokoll simply declared as a "Parliament in Exile".

CHRISTIANE KÜHL

Cargo Sofia, Searching for colleagues in Ljubljana — Photo: Rimini Protokoll

DEUTSCHLAND 2 was just the second project that Helgard Haug, Stefan Kaegi and Daniel Wetzel—who today are still the core of Rimini Protokoll—worked on together, yet the piece demonstrates many traits which have determined the collective to date: involving performers who are not trained actors; an interest in the structures of the world beyond theatre and in the framing of found, non-fictional situations; an explicit disinterest in the illusionary "as-if"; a readiness to tackle questions of presentation and representation; the oscillation of the boundaries between "real" and "unreal," between authentic and manipulated. Nevertheless, in the tremendous body of work which Rimini Protokoll have realised since 2000 (almost 80 productions, all in a wide variation of formats and configurations), two major strands have become identifiable. On one hand there is their conceptual work, which looks outside the theatre space for theatrical situations where they magnify reality and how it is perceived. Such projects include DEUTSCHLAND 2, LOKALTERMIN (ON-SITE INSPECTION, 2003), for which Rimini Protokoll visited court trials in Berlin Moabit with a group of spectators, and HAUPTVERSAMMLUNG (AGM, 2009), for which the group acquired shares of Daimler, in order to attend, with a group of theatre-goers, a twelve-hour meeting of the car corporation's shareholders. On the other hand, Rimini Protokoll also often work inside the classical theatre space, but usually without a basic dramatic text and mostly with people who have never stood on a stage before. It is mainly with this latter approach that Rimini Protokoll have re-invented documentary theatre in the twenty-first century.

Germany has a strong tradition of documentary theatre, such as the work of Erwin Piscator, who was already integrating authentic speeches, pamphlets and newspaper clippings in his work, and Peter Weiss and Rolf Hochhuth, who, in their plays of the sixties, made explicit use of court transcripts as a means of dealing with National Socialism. However, Rimini

CHRISTIANE KÜHL

A LIVE ARCHIVE OF THE EVERYDAY

Protokoll are not interested in the re-enactment of historical events: neither in the re-enactment, nor the historical event itself. Their interest in reality is purely aimed at the everyday and the people who master it, people Rimini Protokoll refer to as "everyday experts". The characteristic feature of Rimini Protokoll is that these people are always on stage in person. Their experience is not embodied by actors, instead they tell their own stories themselves.

By these means a large body of work has accumulated over the years, with long-haul truck drivers, doctors, newscasters or market women, with Brazilian police, Turkish bin men, or Indian call-centre agents as protagonists. In **TORERO PORTERO** (2001) three Argentinean porters share their observations and daily tasks in their apartment building with the audience. In **DEADLINE** (2003) a funeral director, a stone mason, a nurse and an embalmer talk about their work with the dying, the dead and the bereaved. **SABENATION, GO HOME AND FOLLOW THE NEWS** (2004) presents six former employees of the Belgian national airline, two years after its bankruptcy. With Rimini Protokoll, "real people", as they are often misleadingly called, speak directly to the audience and by means of their genuine, unprofessional, physical presence they vouch for the selected fragments of their biographies. It is exactly this non-perfect presentation, the awkward gestures and uncertain speech, which gives the public its proof of authenticity and thereby creates a unique perspective of the stage. And it is this unique perspective, which necessarily creates a changed relationship between stage and audience, which is crucial to the directors:

> That is not the king who is standing up there, it's a person. The person standing there is not someone who has enjoyed four years of training so that he can earn money by being someone else. He is not standing there because he can do something particularly well, which means that one is not distracted by thinking, "Look, how well he can dance!", while you yourself

Cargo Sofia, First Snow in Riga
Photo: Rimini Protokoll

sit there, as a small audience member in the dark. The person standing there is standing there because he is an interesting person. Therefore, you do not ask, "What is the writer trying to tell me?" You ask yourself, "Who is this person?" And you can draw your own conclusions. (STEFAN KAEGI)

It is in this opening up, this permeability, of the stage, both for the audience as well as for the everyday life beyond the theatre, where the political work of Rimini Protokoll takes place. If the old documentary theatre operated as a kind of transmission of a mission, here, the opposite applies, namely in the activity of listening. More than half of the work of the directing/writing trio takes place in the pre-production phase: to begin with there is the lengthy process of the selection of participants, followed by the not-so-simple process of confidence-building between the artists and protagonists, who are new each time and often not familiar with the processes of theatre (or, indeed, the arts in general), followed by a period of interviews. From this material, monologues are written for the individuals, who do not improvise on stage, and then cleverly assembled to create the piece. Stefan Kaegi describes this work as "closer to that of an editor than to that of an author. The stories are already all there. They just need to be selected, framed and given focus." This, however, is somewhat of an understatement, considering the complexity and precision involved in the staging of these stories.

In **CALL CUTTA** (2005) each viewer was equipped with a mobile phone and then personally guided through Berlin by an Indian call-centre employee in Calcutta. The call-centre employees gave the theater-goers directions through a city completely unknown to them. Simultaneously, they told the story of the Indian independence fighter, Subhas Chandra Bose, who came to Berlin in the 1930s to appeal for support from Hitler for his struggle against the British, and the fictional story of their grandfather, who was said to have also been involved in this struggle. Supported by photos and documents which had been placed throughout the city, reality and fiction, past and manipulated-present, overlapped. Meanwhile the remote-controlled walkers began to ponder the new dependencies, conditioned both by globalisation and technological gadgets. In 2008, CALL CUTTA IN A BOX was developed from the aforementioned production, inviting audience members to individually enter an office where they were greeted by the ringing of a telephone. Once again, at the other end of the line, was a call-centre employee in Calcutta, who seemed to know more about your surroundings than you yourself did, and was also able to remotely control the technical devices in the European office space, from the kettle to the computer desktop. More interesting than the question of territorial sovereignty, was the opportunity to get into conversation with a stranger, and in particular to learn about life and working conditions in India from a person whose job often conceals the individual behind the front-line of the service industry. The piece is therefore essentially defined by the encounter, the dramaturgy of which lies to a large extent in the hands of the viewer.

Encounter is an important motif and motive in the work of Rimini Protokoll. "Our work is another way of meeting people, making observations," says Helgard Haug. "We need the discussion, the interaction with people and their biographies. They contribute, even without necessarily realising it, to a huge proportion of the ideas with which we, on the writer/director side of things, construct the project, and in which they then take part." All projects start with a basic theme, but as non-goal-orientated research. Texts are written and rewritten, combined differently or supplemented, often with statistics or video recordings, and so it is only in the course of the work process that the specific topic of the evening materialises. Within this process, everything depends on the balance between the unfamiliar and growing familiarity. Although in extreme cases this has not just been restricted to the practitioners and the performers alone: In RADIO MUEZZIN (2005), a project with Egyptian prayer callers who faced unemployment due to the monopolisation of the prayer callers in Cairo, government censors were also present. With **BODENPROBE KASACHSTAN (EARTH SAMPLE KAZAKHSTAN**, 2011), which deals with the connection between the migration of both oil (as it flows underground) and people in Kazakhstan, the Kazakh Embassy stepped in to make sure that the young state was being represented properly. But representing the bigger picture in a proper way has never been of interest to Rimini Protokoll. Instead the focus is always on individuals who are presented as subjects of history, even if they are intrinsically part of the bigger picture. It is the audience's responsibility to interpret the connections, which, by the very nature of the fragments presented, can be widely varied.

Another problem arises, ironically, when the "actors" become too familiar with their own role—even if it is the role of their own life. The viewer willingly accepts the non-professional feel of the production as long as the performers seem "real". Text uncertainties or misplaced gestures are recognised as proof of "authenticity" and in such a context, come across as very charming. But due to the repetitive nature of rehearsals and performances, the talking-about-oneself loses its naturalness and a non-professional (who, unlike an actor, has never learned repetition) comes across more as an amateur actor than an "everyday expert". The director's task of protecting the protagonists from themselves and any ensuing embarrassment—by means of clear-cut texts and specific activities on the stage—is not to be underestimated. This is in sharp contrast to other reality formats such as television, where protagonists are paraded before an audience, who delight in their nakedness.

Helgard Haug (b.1969), Stefan Kaegi (b.1972) and Daniel Wetzel (b.1969) met while studying Angewandte Theaterwissenschaft (applied theatre studies) at the University of Giessen. The programme, founded in 1982 by Andrzej Wirth, hosts visiting professors such as Marina Abramovic, Eugenio Barba, Heiner Muller, Robert Wilson, Hans-Thies Lehmann (author of the academic standard work, *Postdramatic Theatre*), who connect theory and practice in a unique way. Denounced by the conservative press as "the smithy of misfortune of the German Theatre" (Frankfurter Allgemeine Zeitung), the institute tries and tests performative formats that are recognisably influenced by multimedia and performance art. The work in conventional state theatres was of no interest to Haug, Kaegi and Wetzel during their studies. "For us, then, it was out of the question to think of us working within the institutional system. We did not believe that it was possible to be inspired and work freely within that framework. The theatre had become an educational institution, which was mainly preoccupied with itself." (Helgard Haug). They considered the state theatre, which was then characterised — and to a large extent still is — by psychological theatre, director-led theatre and canonical drama texts, to be highly suspect. This suspicion has even led the group to work with animals as protagonists — because guinea pigs, dogs and ants don't run the risk of falling into the so called "representation traps".

Since 2004, the group's production base has been in the Berlin theatre, Hebbel am Ufer. Their work is funded by the city council of Berlin as well as worldwide co-production partners and a handful of German state theatres who work on a contract basis with the group. That Rimini Protokoll, despite their earlier mistrust of the state theatre system, now work within it, has little to do with a change in their own work as with a huge shift in the state theatre system towards the off-scene and new forms of documentary theatre. This shift could even be said to have been prompted by Rimini Protokoll, whose work in the meantime has been honoured with many awards, including the European Theatre Prize in 2008 under the category, "New Realities." Interestingly, they received two highly prestigious awards, namely an invitation to the Theatertreffen in Berlin and the Mülheim Dramatists Prize, for work which had an existing text at its core, namely WALLENSTEIN — EINE DOKUMENTARISCHE INSZENIERUNG (WALLENSTEIN — A DOCUMENTARY PRODUCTION, 2005) and KARL MARX: DAS KAPITAL, ERSTER BAND (KARL MARX: CAPITAL, VOLUME ONE, 2006). WALLENSTEIN looks for traces of the Schillerian power structures in the biographies of people from East and West Germany; a police director from Weimar meets a politician from Mannheim, Vietnam War veterans meet a former Luftwaffe auxiliary, flanked by an astrologer and a probability researcher. Together they tell of obedience and rebellion in times of political upheaval. KARL MARX: DAS KAPITAL brings together people of different ages and backgrounds, in whose lives the study of Marx has played, or continues to play, a major role. At one point in the show a copy of DAS KAPITAL is distributed to each member of the audience and communally they read excerpts — again a unique occurrence in the German theatre.

The success of Rimini Protokoll is phenomenal. Especially considering the fact that their productions are so "untheatrical" in the traditional sense. They have nothing overwhelming about them and, over time, they are no longer even surprising. In fact, one could even complain about an almost serial production quality, as the basic structure of the pieces is often the same. Exceptions are to be found mainly in relation to the settings, such as in CARGO SOFIA (2006) where the audience were driven around in a truck, which had one side replaced with a sheet of perspex, so that the passing city became a cinematic backdrop for the voice of the Bulgarian truck driver, who spoke from the driver's seat, or in HEUSCHRECKEN (LOCUSTS, 2009) where the spectators were placed around a terrarium with live locusts. But within

A LIVE ARCHIVE OF THE EVERYDAY

these settings, something very similar always takes place: people address the audience face-on with a report of their lives, usually closely related to their occupations. Dialogues between the people on stage do not take place, there is as little action in the dramatic sense, as there is classical dramaturgy, i.e. one with a beginning, a conflict, a climax and catharsis. The people report, the reports are assembled without ideological intent and are then presented by the people themselves. With this format of a new documentary theatre, Rimini Protokoll have made their mark. The success of their work, not only with younger audiences, who are more likely to be open-minded to experiment, but also with the older, "classical" theatre-goers, suggests that they are on the pulse of our time. In a media dominated society whose focus is on sensationalism or the evisceration of the most private, there seems to be a great need for a completely un-sensational, authentic representation of the world (even if the authentic in theatre must necessarily remain fiction).

Interestingly, the world is always presented by Rimini Protokoll in groups: occupational groups, age groups, nationalities, etc. Even if the performers always give subjective information and are never presented as representatives of a community, the viewer gains insight and—due to the nature of theatre—physical contact with a way of life, which they may have been familiar with, but rarely have encountered from such an intimate perspective. This can be seen as a way of creating collective knowledge. In fact, the work of Rimini Protokoll is quite similar to that of a collector, a librarian, an archivist: they choose, group, arrange and display. Within the current tendency of the arts towards the documentary, it is this interest in the concept of the archive which has closely aligned their work to the visual arts. With one significant difference—they don't work with inert artefacts but living people. The work of Rimini Protokoll, in its entirety, creates a contemporary archive: a live archive of the everyday.

CHRISTIANE KÜHL

CHRISTIANE KÜHL

A LIVE ARCHIVE OF THE EVERYDAY 41

Deutschland 2 — Photo: Thilo Beu

CHRISTIANE KÜHL

ESSAY 2

LOLA ARIAS: EXPANDING THE REAL

CECILIA SOSA

ACT 1: A NEW LINEAGE

Saturday night. A committee of trendy youngsters, dressed up in a vintage-modern style, perhaps slightly over-conscious of their intellectual look, gathers at the front of the Centro Cultural Rojas, a public venue that belongs to Buenos Aires University on the sleepless Corrientes Avenue. The occasion is the premiere of **LA ESCUÁLIDA FAMILIA**, Lola Arias's first theatre production. The piece was translated for foreign audiences as **A KINGDOM, A COUNTRY OR A WASTELAND IN THE SNOW**. Arias is 24 and looks like a modern fairy. Her background is already impressive: actress, writer, author of a book of poems entitled *Las Impúdicas (Shameless)*, and a charming series of songs full of fire and weapons. It is October 2001 in Argentina. It is raining heavily and the city centre is flooded with *cartoneros*, those struggling to survive off others' waste, who, after a decade of extreme neo-liberal policies, seem to have fallen beneath the human.

We climb to the stage in half-light and sit on the stands that are just to the side of the set. There is a leaking drip on the stage, reminding us that the premises of the free and massive university may not be the best but they always add a risky charm to the theatrical adventure. In the middle of a chilly landscape there is a fragile building that looks like a house for dolls. It will open up to show the routine of a peculiar family: a father who uses fragments of the Bible to seduce his daughter, a drug-addicted mother who prefers to feed rabbits rather than her own newborn, and two daughters that go hunting in the snow to bring home a hairy orphan boy, almost an idiot, who can barely speak, but who turns out to be the family's abandoned child.

"History is always familiar", writes Arias in the preface to the production.[1] Provocatively, her first production builds a perfect machine for the deconstruction of conventional forms of kinship. Her show turns all possible taboos upside down: twisted Greek myths, cannibalism, zoophilia, parricide and various forms of incest coexist within strands of Herzog's fantasies and Goya's obscure landscapes. Despite the endless unfolding of traumatic events, Arias's production mocks moral premises. In the last scene, Luba—the surviving, pregnant daughter offers her love to Reo, the hairy orphan and prospective husband: "We will found a family of idiots and we will live happily in the end of the snow. We will have one, two, a thousand idiot kids, and we will let them run, love, and die." In the small hall of Buenos Aires University, on a stage almost flooded by rain leaking in from outside, a stylish audience witnesses the foundation of a new lineage: it is a lineage that comes from loss but that presents humour as the extreme form of the tragic.

Two months after Arias's debut, crowds of people took over the streets of Buenos Aires. It is December 2001. While poor rioters loot the supermarkets in the suburbs, a radicalised middle class covers the central squares of the city outraged by the freezing of their bank assets and willing to change the social contract. At the sunset of the insurrectional second day, the helpless President Fernando De la Rúa flies away from the *Pink House* in a helicopter, leaving the country headless in the middle of a colossal crisis.

Arias's post-apocalyptic drama appears to insist that new social ties are needed in contemporary Argentina. It is also the starting point of a wave of young theatre directors who will go on to create a novel circuit in Buenos Aires's theatrical venues. They were mostly born during the dictatorship (1976 – 1983) and could all be vaguely associated with a "post-trauma" generation. The distance that they have gained from loss allows them to see tragedy not only as an opportunity for pain, but also for humour and hope. So, let's let them run and love.

ACT 2: *BELLE DE JOUR*

During the last ten years, Arias has launched a thrilling career that includes theatrical plays, songs, poems, installations, live concerts and urban performances. As a kid, she took lessons in piano, navigation, contemporary dance, writing and swimming. As a teenager, she combined post-structuralist readings for a literature degree and courageous variations on Shakespeare's OTHELLO for her studies in drama. With LA ESCUÁLIDA FAMILIA all these skills began to come together. "I learnt that writing and directing is like having two homes, or being in love with two people at the same time, or living a life with one eye open, and one eye closed," she wrote in a tiny autobiography that was published alongside her TRILOGY.[2]

Drawing from this background, Arias has created a tantalising repertoire that blurs the lines between reality and fiction, poetry and theatre, act and love. She has worked with actors, non-actors, musicians, fish, eggs, dancers, activists, policemen, families of all sorts, babies and even turtles. But Arias's lineage didn't come from nowhere. Along with most of her colleagues, she was nurtured and fed at workshops and seminars run by Ricardo Bartís, Pompeyo Audivert, Mauricio Kartún, Daniel Veronese, Alejandro Tantanián and Rafael Spregelburd, some of the principal lights of the local theatre scene. With a hectic team, Arias co-founded COMPAÑÍA POST-NUCLEAR, which includes a film director (Alejo Moguillansky, b. 1978), a visual artist (Leandro Tartaglia, b. 1977), a dancer and choreographer (Luciana Acuña, b. 1975), and a composer, pianist and free musician (Ulises Conti, b. 1975), with whom she plays live and has released an album. Her "life band", as she refers to her colleagues, also includes other fellow directors and actors such as Federico León, Gerardo Naumann, Mariano Pensotti, Mariana Chaud, Juan Pablo Gomez, and Laura Lopez Moyano. Against the more visible wave of the "New Argentina Cinema", this lineage of theatre-doers runs through an eclectic background. They have created an "off" circuit that offers slightly more sophisticated, stylish and experimental proposals. In a country that has not (yet) been officially conquered by the academic fever of Performance Studies, which is endemic in universities further north, this local theatre community mostly runs without clear rules, reproducing itself as it were backstage, widely and wildly.

Yet, Arias's work has not only reigned locally. Her plays have been presented at international festivals such as Festival Graz, Festival d'Avignon, In Transit Festival Berlin, Spielart Festival Munich and Alkantara Festival Lisboa. Her work has been translated into English, French and German. So what is her appeal?

ACT 3: RECURRING DREAMS

When I first interviewed Arias she had just premiered POSES FOR SLEEPING (2004) at El Camarín de las Musas (The Dressing Room of the Muses), a cult venue in the Abasto district. The name of the venue fitted her well. Arias looked as though she had just bewitched her audience. I could see the spectators walking out of the theatre with mesmerised smiles, as if they were still singing the sweet lyrics sung by four strange creatures as they danced on the last day of the world: a pyromaniac and her husband, and a soldier-girl and her pornographer father; two unconventional couples living next to each other in a futuristic country facing civil war.

At the time Arias said that the piece was about dreams that repeat themselves. Her characters speak another language, one simpler and brighter that recalls the films of Harl Hartley. POSES invents a new vocabulary: that of the "kindem", a sort of porn haiku recited by the girl-soldier—who ignites the passions of the gorgeous pyromaniac. Rather than inhabiting roles, her performers seem to deconstruct them. They could

Parallel Cities — Image supplied by Lola Arias

be German twins, heartbroken suicides, Brazilian policemen, or girl-soldiers. For all of them, roles—as much as fathers and predecessors—are sites of authority that need to be countersigned (in a Derridean sense) and exposed in their own fragility. What comes to the fore is the conviction that humour can be a form of affective reparation that can help to re-inscribe and work through all tragedies. Moreover, there is a conviction that humour can reinvent ties not only on stage but also out of the spotlight, reaching the audience in the darkness. To some extent, she addresses this hope. "There is something beautifully perverse in theatre: some people in darkness, looking at others who laugh, touch themselves, dying," she says.[3] This is the liminal ethics that animates her work, a form of doing that calls attention to how relationships are made and re-made both on and off the stage.

ACT 4: MAKING IT PERSONAL

"The autobiographical is not the personal," writes Lauren Berlant at the beginning of *The Female Complaint*.[4] Arias also shows how the fragile material that informs privates lives can emerge as a screen for broader publics. For her, personal stories can work as a delicate medium of transmitting affective experiences between stage and the audience.

In Arias's work the "substance" of this sharing acquires different forms. Within TRILOGY (2007), a three-part study on love, she imposes dramatic tests on her audiences. Responding to the London Royal Court Theatre's request for a play on "violence and the city", Arias came up with SUEÑO CON REVOLVER (REVOLVER DREAMS). Far from a third-world postcard of poverty she staged the beginning of a sneaky love story between a drug-dealing teacher and a teenager. But with a catch: the audience was left in total shadow and had to follow the encounter through a slim gap in the curtain. "I thought that the best way of representing violence was leaving the spectators in darkness," she argued.[5] In the 1990s the city of Buenos Aires was periodically without electricity and people routinely carried buckets of water to their homes, staggering like melancholic sleepwalkers. As if playing on those hypnotic days, Arias left her helpless spectators to scrutinise fragments of naked bodies and voices through the shadows of what might be read as a power cut. A rare intimacy emerges between the actors and the public, a form of sharing less like conventional theatre and more like those blissful conversations that come in darkness just before sleep.

The second part was **STRIPTEASE**, a piece with a baby as the main character. Here the challenge was different. Audiences had to hold their breath and manage their own anxieties while following the movement of a little creature playing, crying, eating, throwing a plastic toy from a cradle, or carrying it around like her own living world. By then, the quarrel of the young parents at the front of the stage becomes a murmur, almost the off-stage voice of a text written by a baby. Arias spent months until she found two actresses willing to play the mother. "The rehearsals were a jump in the void", says the director.[6] It was no less daunting for the audience. What if the baby suddenly discovers all those strangers staring at her in the darkness? Or if she simply starts crying and ruins the whole play? But wait…is there anything else to "ruin"? As Arias puts it, a baby on stage says nothing but "this is not theatre".[7] In fact, this edgy choreography makes spectators more self conscious than ever of their own bodily presence abandoned in the dark.

EL AMOR ES UN FRANCOTIRADOR (LOVE IS A SNIPER) provides a pop art closing to this **TRILOGY**. Staged by the Postnuclear Company, the show features a Russian Roulette game in which a group of six suicidal people pronounce their last will and testament before shooting themselves. The players follow almost fixed roles: the shy guy, the beauty, the boxer, the cowgirl, the Don Juan, the stripper. In each performance one of them dies. While monologues, songs, dreams and kisses circulate on stage a garage band plays live. Within this tragic but still pop-surreal atmosphere, the final show does not deny the biographies of the actors. In fact, this fictional community of suicides prefigures another community, that of six actors whose real lives will be staged in **MY LIFE AFTER** (2009), by far Arias's most startling and contested piece.

ACT 5: A KISS IN A TIME MACHINE

A cascade of clothes falls onto an empty stage. A woman in her early twenties comes out from the mountain of fabric and picks out a pair of jeans. She puts them on and says to the audience: "Twenty years later I find a pair of my mum's jeans from the seventies, and they fit me just right. I put on the jeans and start to walk towards the past." The whole play works as a time machine. As if it were a science-fiction film, six professional actors dress as their parents, remaking episodes of their past lives. This documentary of memory draws from the real experiences of these actors born during the dictatorship. They are descendants of guerrilla activists and exiled intellectuals. There is the son of a bank employee, and the son of a priest, the daughter of a military intelligence officer who stole a newborn baby from a detained activist couple.

In Argentina, the network of organisations created by the victims of state terrorism followed the trope of a "wounded family". Seemingly, only those related by blood to the missing had the authority to claim for justice. Decoupled from traditional discourses, Arias's production playfully engages with family pictures, letters, old toys and a turtle — purported to have the gift of prophesy — which has been inherited by one of the actors (In each performance, the creature signals

"YES" or "NO" to predict whether or not there will be a revolution in the country.) The show subverts the boundaries between documentary and fiction, the private and the collective. When it was re-staged in 2011 in Buenos Aires, MY LIFE AFTER aroused heated debates. A well-known critic accused the play of trivialising the conflicts of the past.[8] In a period in which the national government adopted memory as an official duty, Arias's production calls into question the legitimacy of remembering in the aftermath of violence.

Arias does not have any "disappeared" relatives. "Journalists kept on asking why I wanted to tell this story. I was born in 1976 [the year of the military coup], and all my childhood was marked by violence, *how* I could not be affected?", she once told me. Her piece adopts the right of precisely those who are not usually considered "victims". It stands for a technology of memory in which loss is not limited to familial borders but open to more expanded affiliations.

While enacting different versions of an activist's death, or remaking the kiss of an exiled couple as if it were part of a cheesy TV soap opera, the bodies of the actors recreate a generational platform for the transmission of trauma. They displace the monopoly of suffering while bringing on stage new desires emerged from grief. MY LIFE AFTER highlights the sensuousness of this encounter, an encounter between the artefact and the flesh, between laughter and a pair of jeans that comes as a gift from the past. This encounter also resonates through the bodies of the audience, suggesting a new sense of being together after loss.

ACT 6: PARALLEL LIVES

August 2011. Arias lives in Berlin. Her recent work has become more and more transnational. Nonetheless, it still explores more fluid conceptions of the family. In FAMILIENBANDE

(2009), an 11-year-old girl from a little German village tells how if it feels living with a father and two mothers, and a brother who is the son of her father and her second mother. "It sounds complicated but it is not", contends the girl. As a counter token, in **THAT ENEMY WITHIN** (2010) two identical twins interrogate the limits of blood through their own experiences in theatre.

And there is more. With Stefan Kaegi, her partner in life and work and also a founding member of the cutting-edge Rimini Protokoll Company, Arias has crafted her most ambitious project: **PARALLEL CITIES** (2010—2011). After producing an installation with Brazilian policemen in Sao Paulo, **CHÁCARA PARAÍSO: ART POLICE EXHIBITION** (2007), and engaging with nomad children in **AIRPORT KIDS** (2008), the artistic couple transform entire cities into venues. **PARALLEL CITIES** takes place successively in Buenos Aires, Warsaw, Zurich, and Copenhagen. In each case, local artists are invited to devise interventions for public spaces. The venues are malls, train stations, libraries, hotels and factories; spaces that "live parallel existences around the world" and are compelled to show their local faces. The public may be invited to climb a terrace in the centre of Buenos Aires following the instructions of a blind man to contemplate a stunning sunset, to visit a hotel in Copenhagen in order to have a one-on-one chat with the maid in charge of the room service, or to travel to the margins of a city in order to participate in a factory assembly line. Or it could be just to witness how the thoughts of random passengers become magically displayed on gigantic screens at a railway station anywhere in the world. In all these cases, cities become "targets" that create not only new experiences but also new audiences. Ultimately, what is tested in **PARALLEL CITIES** is the possibility of finding other forms of recognition among strangers, when familiar spaces become the stage for unexpected encounters.

CECILIA SOSA

LOLA ARIAS: EXPANDING THE REAL

THE CURTAIN NEVER COMES DOWN

"Real lives", "testimony", and "experience:" these are the latest obsessions of contemporary theatre. In dealing with them, some performers manage to make visible something that was not there before. They managed to build new life on stage. Arias shows how performance is nothing but a *doing*, a form of creating affective relations inside a library, a rail station or any random stage where a team sings a cheesy song, or a family devours itself. Throughout her work, Arias has created *life* on stage.

Both her fictional and documentary pieces propose an expansion of reality. They bring to light a new collection of intensities for the intimate public sphere. In some sense, Arias's affective installations reframe intimacy. Or better, they make intimacy theatrical. Her performances show how the lives that we feel most authentically and ethically involved with are precisely those that we perceive when we are in a "spectatorial position."[9]

Arias's work does not respond to scripts but to experiences. Her performances are experimental laboratories where alternative lives are tested and composed. In different ways, they all show other ways of being together. They are miniatures of parallel worlds. They can travel towards the past, or towards the future. They can resemble time machines or surreal poems. In any case, they stage other forms of conviviality: fleeting communities, taking place here and there. Within this titillating collection, life becomes expanded and theatre is reinvented once and again.

1. Arias, Lola *La Escuálida Familia* (2001), Buenos Aires: Ed Libros del Rojas, p.38
2. Arias, Lola *Striptease, Sueño con revólver, El amor es un francotirador*—1ª ed.—Buenos Aires: Entropía, 2007, p.79
3. In the original: "Hay algo hermosamente perverso en el tea tro: algunas personas a oscuras, observan a otros riendo, tocándose, muriendo" (my translation). See Arias, *La Escuálida Familia*, p.45
4. Berlant, Lauren *The Female Complaint*, vii
5. Arias, *Striptease*, p.80
6. Arias, *Striptease*, p.84
7. Arias, *Striptease*, p.84
8. Villalba, Susana "El discurso del vencedor," Revista N, February 12, 2011
9. L. Berlant, p.181

LOLA ARIAS: EXPANDING THE REAL

My Life After – Image supplied by Lola Arias

CECILIA SOSA

ESSAY 3

THEATRE REMINDS ME OF POLITICS

JACOB WREN

ONE

In Tim Lawrence's book *Love Saves The Day: A History of American Dance Music Culture, 1970—1979*, there was one anecdote that particularly fascinated me. In 1965, when the New York club Shephard's replaced its house band with a DJ, the American Federation of Musicians picketed in protest. "We are in direct competition with the discotheque recordings that are used publicly for profit," a union official told the New York Times. "Therefore we have a right to place pickets wherever those recordings are played. The managements of places depending on live music also feel that the discotheque is giving them unfair competition."[1]

This story reflects many of my questions and artistic concerns. Is there something fundamentally different between the experience of going to see a live band and listening to a recording? Are there some essential attributes that make a performance situation "live", and if so how do they differ from attributes of recorded media? Is a live experience more intense? More real? More immediate? More unexpected? I don't have precise answers for any of these questions, but it's my hope that contemporary performance will continue to struggle with them.

In the above anecdote the DJ is literally putting the musicians out of work. (In such matters I always side with the union, but can't fail to admit I love, and perhaps even prefer, listening to records.) It also suggests a certain dynamic between the individual and the community: the musicians cooperate with each other, they work, play (and in this case picket) together, while the DJ spins alone.

As we now know, the future was in many ways on the DJ's side. We live in a world in which we are constantly surrounded by mediated experiences: photographs, television, movies, music, internet, advertising of every kind. I have often wondered if making a live performance might offer alternative ways of watching and of being together, ways that differ significantly from watching a movie, being on the internet or even dancing to a DJ. And then I wonder if the "liveness" of the experience might in some ways be implicitly political, since being together with other people is always the first step towards politics. (The second step being when a large enough number of people all agree to push in the same direction).

TWO

When I say that theatre reminds me of politics what I mean, more specifically, is that theatre reminds me of the current state of the left. It's a shaggy, fumbling (perhaps slightly paranoid) metaphor, but it's one that continues to resonate for me. It is not the result of a detailed historical analysis but rather a feeling that has gradually accumulated over the past twenty years of professional experience.

From my perspective what happens, over and over, is that some new energy arises, a push towards different ways of making and thinking about theatre. This new energy, after being partially absorbed by the more traditional approach, is then substantially suppressed. This is why, in theatre, to direct conventional productions of Shakespeare is still considered a respectable career path, while in visual art, for example, to earnestly paint works in the style of Rembrandt would be considered ridiculous.

In the nineties the anti-globalisation movement was really picking up steam. It felt like something might genuinely begin to change, that convincing forms of global resistance were rapidly emerging. Then the protests in Seattle and Genoa happened, protesters died, and, especially since 9/11, new counter-terrorism laws have been freely used against anti-globalisation activists, severely impeding their movement and efficacy. A surge of radical energy that doesn't last long before it is effectively suppressed. On a local level, in different countries and various contexts, I believe something analogous happens in theatre on an ongoing basis.

Perhaps this pattern of absorption and suppression has something to do with a fight over the definition of what theatre is. Is theatre primarily a question of history: a desire, expressed in terms of craft, to ensure that significant traditions are kept alive and have their place? Or is it a contemporary art form struggling to fully engage with modernity, with everything that's come since and with the future? We live in pluralist times, so most might answer that it is simultaneously both. Of course, since art is subjective, this must in some sense be the case. But the failure of more contemporary forms of theatre to find a consistent place within the larger world of the art form leads me to speculate that more is going on here. We cannot have both socialism and capitalism, at least not when up against a form of tenacious, neoliberal market ideology that insists that consumers, transactions and profit are the only game in town.

THREE

Much like in radical politics, for me the most consequent contemporary theatre is that which deals with the immediate, concrete situation. By the concrete situation, I mean that the performers are in the same room with the audience, that they are not in a different location, not on the other side of a movie camera in a different space and time. We are all right here, sharing an as-yet only partly defined space.

One might say this is the case with all theatre. But I believe that most often, in service of a story or particular aesthetic,

Individualism Was A Mistake
by PME-ART, Photo: David Jacques

actors perform as if they are in another world and audiences watch them as if they are watching a movie. Much like celluloid, rehearsal and repetition are also recording mediums. That a theatre show is the same every night, regardless of the moods of the performers or the energy of the audience, suggests a situation—much like a film after picture and sound are locked—that cannot be changed.

How to make it feel like the world is not completely fixed? That we all have some modicum of power to change the things that most affect us? How, in a performance, to make it feel like we are all together in the same space? How to honestly face the inherently fragile, vulnerable nature of the situation?

There is an understandable impulse, on the part of the performer, to protect themselves: through virtuosity, excessive preparation, technology, performative flourish, etc. There is the impulse to differentiate themselves from the other people in the room, from the audience, as much as possible. This impulse might also be viewed as a desire, influenced by fear, to distance themselves from what is most immediate, to defuse the intimacy and potential for conflict and in doing so undermine what is really at stake.

Here we might use the example of a politician during an election campaign. Is the politician only trying to get your vote, her words simply propaganda towards that aim? Or is she attempting to engage with people whose lives will be affected by her decisions and by the policies she enacts? These are clearly different attitudes that entail different modes of thinking and presentation. If I am only trying to get your vote, if I have already decided how I am going to govern before our encounter begins, then I will naturally deflect all criticism. (They called Reagan "the Teflon president"). But if I am attempting to genuinely engage, to discover, through

Individualism Was A Mistake by PME-ART, Photo: David Jacques

the situation, what is most required, then I am in a considerably more vulnerable position, constantly having to place my own principles in relation to the demands of those I am speaking with. When I am criticised I must take the criticisms into account, consider whether they are valid, search for the compromises and moments of mutual understanding that might eventually lead to small breakthroughs. At every juncture it could all go wrong. There are no guarantees. This more vulnerable approach contains a much greater potential for engagement, but also a greater possibility of failure.

Of course art is not a democracy and performers are not beholden to any specific constituency. Nonetheless, how one thinks of the performance situation has a substantial impact on what a performance can mean. On the most literal level we might say that an actor's understandable desire to protect themselves, to make themselves look good at all costs, is really only the fear of not pleasing the audience, or of not being understood (and therefore not accepted). However, on a more subtle and counter-intuitive level I believe it is also a fear of being understood too much, of connecting too directly and intimately, a connection that one senses is false (and even empty) because when the show is over all connection is severed as the performers and audience go their separate ways.

Everyone who works in theatre must, at some point, ask themselves what courage might mean in a contemporary performance situation. There is much spectacular work around today, work that uses nudity and violence to generate a visceral or emotional effect. And when I watch such work it is always at the forefront of my mind that capital loves a spectacle.

FOUR

The desire for theatre to be a contemporary art form may well have a paradox lodged at the heart of it. Cinema, television, video and the internet are all more contemporary forms. In many ways theatre was a precursor to cinema. Cinema and television are the art forms that have supplanted theatre as socially central, widely cared about, mediums for performed storytelling. In a larger cultural sense we might say that theatre is a more old-fashioned form of movies and therefore cannot be contemporary. However, alongside the frustration of feeling outmoded, this historical reality brings about many unexpected opportunities. Since cinema is a medium effortlessly capable of much greater verisimilitude, it frees theatre from its need to mirror reality, opening a world of near infinite possibility.

In his essay "What Is The Contemporary"?, Italian philosopher Giorgio Agamben suggests that to be contemporary actually means to be untimely, to be out of sync with the time in which one lives. He quotes from *Untimely Meditations*, in which Nietzsche writes that his book is untimely because it "seeks to understand as an illness, a disability, and a defeat something which this epoch is quite rightly proud of." Agamben goes on to suggest that being contemporary requires "a singular relationship with one's own time, which adheres to it and, at the same time, keeps a distance from it. More precisely, it is *that relationship with time that adheres to it through a disjunction and an anachronism*."[2]

In his essay "Critical Reflections," the Russian art critic Boris Groys suggests that, in the 1920s, Russian avant-garde artists were in fact making art for a new kind of man who did not yet exist, for the new man that the revolution would bring into existence. They were making art for those who did not yet exist, but they were making it in the present, forcing a choice upon the viewer: either he could side with the art and be a part of the future, or he could side with the present and be against the art (and in the view of the artists eventually be left behind). Groys writes:

> The art of the avant-garde consciously withdrew itself from the judgement of the public. It did not address the public as it was but instead spoke to a new humanity as it should—or at least could—be. The art of the avant-garde presupposed a different, new humanity for its reception—one that would be able to grasp the hidden meaning of pure colour and form (Kandinsky), to subject its imagination and even its daily life to the strict laws of geometry (Malevich, Mondrian, the Constructivists, Bauhaus), to recognise a urinal as a work of art (Duchamp). The avant-garde thus introduced a rupture in society not reducible to any previously existing social differences.[3]

These questions of the contemporary have a particular resonance for theatre and performance. When Nietzsche was writing his untimely meditations he could believe he was writing for the future, but a performance, in one sense, is always happening now. We might say that for a performance, when it's really happening, there is no future. This aspect, implicit in all live art, resonates strangely with our experience of the early twenty-first century, since today it often seems like we no longer believe in the future, or at least not in a positive one. There is the frequently quoted Frederick Jameson quip that it is "easier for us to imagine the end of the world than it is to imagine an end to capitalism." And yet being reminded of the potency of the present—the effect of every good performance—has the potential to open up the future once again, to help us understand why it might be worth pursuing. When we envision the future as apocalyptic, in a sense we are also suggesting that life is not meaningful enough now, and therefore not worth saving.

For a performance to be contemporary in Agamben's sense, for it to be in disjunction with the present, might also mean that it is never properly seen, or, at the very least, that it will not receive the acclaim that it might if it were to survive into the future like a book or film.

FIVE

I am writing this text at a precarious moment in my professional life. For the last twelve years I have been co-artistic director of the Montreal performance group PME-ART and now, for the first time, we feel forced to consider shutting down. We have received sporadic funding over the past twelve years, often surviving through extensive touring in Europe, and this year we received almost nothing. We're exhausted, frayed, wondering how to keep going and what might still be possible. Maybe we'll survive or maybe we won't. At the moment I genuinely don't know, and wonder if I still care. Or in what way I should care. Twelve years of trying to make work radically unlike anything else out there (whether or not this is a noble goal) has left me feeling completely lost.

So in writing that theatre reminds me of the failures of the left, I suddenly find myself wondering if I am engaging in a kind of covert autobiography? Or in self-fulfilling prophecy? Do I think that defeat is inevitable because we are in the process of being defeated, or are we in the process of being defeated because I believe defeat is inevitable? (Or will we simply survive?)

Of course, PME-ART certainly isn't the only arts organisation struggling with questions of survival these days. As we know, arts funding is being heavily cut in many countries as right wing governments place the market, and occasionally war or religion, above all else. This is neoliberalism at work, privatising everything so the money trickles upwards to the richest one per cent, and, in the face of its overwhelming victories, arts cuts are possibly the least of our worries. But the failure of the left to find new, visionary ways to fight against neoliberalism often merges in my feverish, paranoid brain with my own failure to have a greater impact on my local theatre context, or on theatre in general.

This is one of the things artists do: we find parallels between personal experiences and larger social realities. I find myself mulling over the past twelve years, replaying all the mistakes we have made, wondering what might have happened if PME-ART had been more strategic or more perfect. Would we be in better shape today? This is also how neoliberalism works. It's up to you to fend for yourself, your difficulties are no one's fault but your own. In Montreal over the past twenty years the cultural funding has steadily flowed up towards the largest organisations. Our struggle is part of a more general pattern and yet, so often, we feel we are fighting alone.

These moments of professional uncertainty, of precarity, mirror the qualities I often find most beautiful in performance. I love it in a performance when something goes wrong, when the performers experience real difficulty and are honest in their struggle, when you feel the entire thing could topple at any moment. This preference is possibly another form of self-fulfilling prophecy.

SIX

The festival circuit is simultaneously the exception to, and enforcement of, what I mean when I say that theatre reminds me of politics. The festival circuit pulls things out of their local context and places them on the international stage. Local companies pushing hard at the boundaries of their art form, if they are successful, often find themselves with heavy touring schedules. This is globalisation as it relates to the performing arts. A heavy touring schedule is generally seen as a clear sign of success, but the matter is considerably more complex. When you pull yourself away from the local context, over time, it becomes increasingly difficult to intertwine one's artistic perspective with that of the local community. It begins to feel like conventional theatre is local, and adventurous theatre is international, and the more one is away, on the road, the harder it is to build bridges between them.

Most artists and groups taking artistic risks meet one of three fates: either they are unable to continue (due to lack of support and/or performance opportunities), they find their way onto an international circuit, or they drift towards making more conventional work. (Many artists might not choose this more conventional path if there wasn't considerable pressure to do so.) All of these options emphasise that artistic experimentation is not a normal, acceptable way of making theatre. It's an exception and must be treated as such.

SEVEN

Historically, the left (and radical left) has certainly had its share of problems. Infighting and factionalism have been rampant, while an emphasis on personal freedoms perhaps fit too neatly with the requirements of advertising and consumerism. And yet without an effective left-wing presence everything simply drifts further and further to the right. Without anything concrete to back it up, critique gradually becomes meaningless. The left today finds itself at a considerable impasse. In her introduction to the book *Capital and its Discontents*, the American writer and radio broadcaster Sasha Lilley summarises the situation:

> Capitalist neoliberalism has undermined the basis for organizing in myriad ways. Neoliberalism has meant a gloves-off form of class war, borne out by the assault on militant unions,

relentless restructuring of employment, speed up, wage slashing, and intentional unemployment as a means of disciplining workers and breaking organised labor. [...]

Yet neoliberalism has operated in other ways, which are subtler, but no less destructive. The enormous growth of finance over the past three decades and the integration of the working class into financial circuits, through pensions, mortgage, and credit card debt, have bound people into the system In the US, students—often a constituency of the left—must take part- or full-time jobs to pay their tuition and expenses while they are studying. Upon graduation, they are burdened with such high levels of debt that they typically choose jobs that will allow them to pay their financial obligations, rather than opting for avenues that would be more conducive to political engagement and activism.

A working class that is debt-ridden, deeply incorporated into the circuits of finance, increasingly atomised, forced out of public spaces that have been enclosed, divided by racism and lacking the social supports and time to engage with each other is at a distinct disadvantage in facing the assaults of capital or organising in its own interest. Its members often lack the wherewithal to, as E.P. Thompson phrased it, "identify points of antagonistic interest...commence to struggle around these issues and in the process of struggling...discover themselves as [a] class."[4]

Yet even if the obstacles were less ferocious, solidarity is rare. Freud speaks of "the narcissism of small differences," how the greater your similarities are with another individual or group the more fiercely you will obsess over the differences. If I really am different from you, or in a distinct social role, I won't need to do much to prove it. But if we are basically doing the same thing my individuality is threatened, and I will push to establish my significance. Focusing on small differences likely means not working to find the similarities that might, over time, grow into a common cause.

Artists, at their worst, pray at the altar of these small differences and the competition that ensues. This is a serious enough problem, but it is not quite where my "theatre reminds me of politics" finds its weakest link. Because even when artists do manage to engage in effective acts of solidarity, for example to protest funding cuts, it is difficult to imagine how such solidarity might be used not for practical ends but instead to support ongoing idiosyncratic risk-taking. While clearly unionists or activists might some day engage in serious collective resistance in order to improve their daily conditions, and there is a rich history of such resistance to draw upon, it is much harder to know how artists could utilise similar collective strategies in order to make their respective art forms more complex or vital.

This shortcoming is somewhat beside the point. It is too literal. My analogy hinges on theatre and leftist politics sharing similar shades of idealism. The dream that things could be different. Trying to shift reality closer to hopes that are still in the process of being defined. Always struggling with the emotional triage of defeat. When faced with insurmountable odds, the only real choice is to find some way to keep going, to cling tight to the truth that the way things are will not always be the case, the world is constantly changing, and our actions have consequences.

EIGHT

It would be difficult to compile a comprehensive history of all the valuable artists and groups that have disappeared, or felt pressured into a more conventional approach, over the past fifty or one hundred years. (And by what standards would we judge?) Without such a history my central thesis must

Individualism Was A Mistake
by PME-ART, Photo: David Jacques

remain speculation. While I definitely think of it as an ongoing concrete reality, it is also a metaphor for how challenging it is to remain artistically consequent making contemporary theatre over the course of a lifetime. What makes it most challenging is how ephemeral performance is. Documentation aside, without being able to see and consider all the breakthroughs that have been made over the past hundred or so years it is impossible to place one's practice in an accurate artistic and historical context. There's a lot of re-inventing the wheel in contemporary performance.

Something I often notice in critical theory is how much easier it is to identify and brilliantly analyse the many problems of the world than it is to propose anything resembling solutions. Analysis of problems seems accurate and convincing (and depressing) while proposed solutions often seem weak and ineffective in comparison. I often wonder if this is a problem with the world or actually a more schematic problem that has to do with almost mythological aspects of language. How writing something negative and apocalyptic seems so much more compelling than writing something civil or, for example, about having more community meetings. (Or, in relation to theatre, about having better theatre schools and audience development programs.)

Around the time I was starting to write this text I was also following the teachers protests in Wisconsin (which began in February 2011). Every new surge of the capitalist right seems to begin with breaking a union (Thatcher breaking the Coal Miners Union, Reagan breaking the Air Traffic Controllers), but breaking a teachers' union has an enormous symbolic resonance that I find heartbreaking. It is like saying we don't care about the next generation, the future can take care of itself. (Or, more accurately, we only care about those in the next generation rich enough to afford private schools.)

THEATRE REMINDS ME OF POLITICS

As I was watching what was in fact an enormous and inspiring act of solidarity—between 70,000 and 100,000 protesting the Wisconsin Budget Repair Bill that would eventually eliminate collective bargaining rights for public employees—I found myself thinking that someday in the future the fight would have to begin again. Everything that was once fought for, and gained, was being lost, and someday it would all have to be redone from scratch. There are many different reasons and necessities for reinventing the wheel.

In contemporary performance the need to perpetually start over is obviously not as dire. There is even a certain creative urgency to be gained through starting from scratch, returning to core questions, to the beginning. In a sense, since the modernist breaks of the twentieth century, every time one makes a new work one is asking what is art today and why. Nonetheless, I genuinely find myself asking what the contemporary theatre landscape might look like if more artists were able to build on the full richness of the experimental legacy. And, within a multitude of local contexts, if the most audacious artists were less frequently brushed aside.

In such predicaments what does it mean to fight? Or to fight effectively? If I knew, I like to believe I would be doing more, either in theatre or in politics, wherever it would help most. It makes me crazy that I don't know what to do, what the next step might be. That I feel so lost.

Then I wonder to what extent my confusion embodies the current historical moment, and to what extent such confusion has always been the case. For example, "And I Always Thought," the last poem by Bertolt Brecht. He was also drowning in world historical uncertainty and yet had access to perspectives and convictions that now feel much harder to embody. He is an uncanny example of everything mentioned above. Though certainly famous enough, outside of

Germany his ideas about how to make and think about theatre are rarely, and not thoroughly, explored. They are vaguely understood and only sporadically considered essential. This was his last poem:

> And I always thought: the very simplest words
> Must be enough. When I say what things are like
> Everyone's heart must be torn to shreds.
> That you will go down if you don't stand up for yourself
> Surely you see that.

1. Lawrence, Tim *Love Saves The Day: A History of American Dance Music Culture*, 1970 –1979 (Durham, NC: Duke University Press Books, 2004) p.14–15
2. Agamben, Giorgio "What Is The Contemporary?", in *Nudities* (Palo Alto, CA: Stanford University Press, 2010) p.41
3. Groys, Boris "Critical Reflections," *Art Power* (Cambridge, MA: The MIT Press, 2008) p.112
4. Lilley, Sasha "Introduction," *Capital and Its Discontents: Conversations with Radical Thinkers in a Time of Tumult* (Oakland, CA: PM Press/Spectre, 2011) p.12–14

Wondering at the mouth of a geyser in Iceland
Photo © Philippe Quesne

ESSAY 4

PHILIPPE QUESNE'S VIVARIUM STUDIO: A VIEWER'S VIEWS

Bivouac, Vivarium Studio/Collection Conséquences — Photo © Philippe Quesne

DENISE LUCCIONI

[PHOTO BIVOUAC]
[CLOSE-UP]

Do you feel the cold in the night, the boat rolling? Do you know where you are, or where you are going? Are you afraid? Or are you just standing on the bank, wondering? And if you are on the bank, can you feel the boat rolling?

[ZOOM OUT]

You can tell this is a photograph. You are not drifting in the night and the fog, inside a bright yellow inflatable boat along a mysterious stream, you are sitting at home or on a bus, browsing through **NO MORE DRAMA**.

You are experiencing how a typical Vivarium Studio performance operates on the audience, whether a stage production, a site-specific event or a booklet, like the one this photo comes from.

You are the photographed as well as the photographer and the viewer: the actor and the witness. You are required to use your eyes, your sensorial imagination, your sense of association, your memory...Given the opportunity to widen your perception, you are on the road to ubiquity.

This is no ordinary image, one of the countless made by theatre. What is shown here is really happening. And the photo can reverberate diversely, from picturing a simple action to providing a prosaic version of a myth. It is about drawing a path made of signs for spirits to see. Magic? Yes, embodied, acted out. You are taken on a voyage in and out of the photo, beyond imagery, beyond theatre, deep into reality.

No speech, no character, no plot. No beginning, no ending—timeless. A snapshot, a slice of life skipping into an-

DENISE LUCCIONI

other dimension. Being or distributing signs in a landscape, on the walls of a cave, you are a part of this, you are both the shadows in the photo and the viewers in the dark.

[ETYMOLOGIES & DEFINITIONS]

Vivarium:
An enclosure (often a glass case) [...] prepared for keeping animals under semi-natural conditions for observation or study [...]. From Latin "vivere," *"to live."*

Studio:
[...] A room where an artist [...] works; a place where performers [...] practice [...]; a place where movies are made [...]. From Latin "studium," *"study."*

Drama:
A play for theatre, radio, or television; [...] an emotional set of circumstances. From Greek [...] "dran," *"to do, act, perform."*

Theatre:
From Greek "theasthai," *"to behold."*

Poetry:
Work in which special intensity is given to the expression of feelings and ideas by the use of distinctive style and rhythm. From Greek "poieo," *"I create."*

[SE NON È VERO, È BENE TROVATO]

PLATO'S ALLEGORY OF THE CAVE

"Socrates describes a group of people who have lived chained to the wall of a cave all of their lives, facing a blank wall. They watch shadows projected on the wall by things passing in front of a fire behind them. According to Socrates,

DENISE LUCCIONI

the shadows are as close as the prisoners get to viewing reality. The philosopher is like a prisoner who is freed from the cave and comes to understand that the shadows on the wall do not make up reality at all, as he can perceive the true form of reality rather than the mere shadows seen by the prisoners." (Thank You, Wikipedia)

HORACE WALPOLE'S THE CASTLE OF OTRANTO

In this first "gothic" novel, a series of inexplicable events occur in a castle, starting with Lord Manfred's son being killed on his wedding day by a gigantic helmet falling on him in the courtyard. Huge pieces of a statue then regularly drop from the sky, wreaking havoc, ominously related to an ancient prophecy: "The lordship of Otranto should pass from the present family, whenever the real owner should be grown too large to inhabit it." The influence of religion is felt everywhere, angelic women get stabbed in dark churches, or underground passages and the like. The ending is not happy.

[A BRIEF HISTORY]

Philippe Quesne was trained in visual arts. Where was he trained to question "theatre"? His graduation production unexpectedly connected Maeterlinck's book *The Life of the Termite* and Beckett's novella *The Lost Ones*. He could have chosen the performing arts arena right away, but he started designing for theatre, opera and exhibitions instead. In 2003, he founded his company Vivarium Studio, and produced LA DÉMANGEAISON DES AILES (ITCHING OF WINGS), which was rehearsed in an apartment with a group of friends and a dog. The piece attracted immediate attention. Vivarium started touring abroad. At the time, most French venues still grinned sarcastically at this type of multimedia work. It just didn't fit with any notion of French culture. Today, Vivarium regularly travels around the world. L'EFFET DE SERGE (THE SERGE

DENISE LUCCIONI

EFFECT), already performed almost 150 times in more than 15 countries, got an Obie in New York in 2010. In France, "consecration" often coincides with presentations at the official Avignon Festival. Vivarium has featured in the festival twice, with **THE MELANCHOLY OF DRAGONS**, then **BIG BANG**.

Why was it easier for foreigners to accept Vivarium Studio right away? Because Vivarium might be described as "No More (French) Drama"; it is not based on text or a certain type of delivery and acting. In other words, for foreign audiences, Vivarium came as a refreshing surprise, proving at the same time terribly French but different from everything that is expected from the French. Being praised abroad before being accepted at home has shaped a modus operandi for the company, which has been developing "organically" along post-capitalist modes of production: in other words, ones that resist grand styles and global proportions. Or is it that a love for handmade, homemade, human scales led them to resist capitalist modes?

[ITCHING OF WINGS, THE AGENDA]

Most notions key to Vivarium's work were formulated from this first piece about flying, juxtaposing live action and short filmed interviews. The title, borrowed from Plato, is explained in the first filmed interview: the backs of lovers itch, where the wings of love are growing. The audience walks through the set and performing area to get to their seats, thus enabled to contemplate a bric-a-brac of props, or one actor already lying on a mattress, erasing barriers between stage and house. A bibliography listed out loud provides context and cues — from technical treatises by Leonardo to Perec's **A MAN ASLEEP**. In a visual reference to art, a performer attempts to reproduce Brueghel's **FALL OF ICARUS** — this reminder of the human condition suggesting, perhaps, other ways to fly?

DENISE LUCCIONI

Filmed interviews (with a philosophy teacher, a dentist and model-building obsessive, a *Taiji* addict, an anarchist songwriter, a reader of Gilles Deleuze) grant their documentary support to the venture.

Technology is featured by found cheap sci-fi objects, such as an out-of-order computer in the role of a visibly fake motion-capture contraption and earphones and projections on a bare wall. And wireless mics. A guest rock band appears, plays a set and leaves. For economic reasons, ITCHING didn't tour with the original group but picked up local musicians at each stop.

No explanation is given to relate any of the events to each other. The title is our only link. Obviously, each item, itself an entry unveiling its agenda, leads into a maze, or a rhizomatic structure.

[SOMETIMES, A CIGAR IS JUST A CIGAR...]

Up to a certain point in time, titles say it all and give a thread, a string of words making sense *per se* and as a sequence. As if they were scores or to-do lists. Words and formulae were always essential to magic; in those titles, each word has the weight of a performative action.

After ITCHING OF WINGS, the company's initial take off, DES EXPÉRIENCES (EXPERIMENTS, 2004) offers a series of...well, guess! Then comes a first booklet, ACTIONS IN NATURAL ENVIRONMENTS (2005), featuring photographs of these experiments, leading to D'APRÈS NATURE (FROM LIFE OR TRUE TO LIFE, 2006), a production which is poised between nature and society. The stage is literally divided into two parts; nature, stage left, planted with a forest where performers grope in semi-darkness or blindness, and a kitchen or dining room, stage right, where they cook and sing.

DENISE LUCCIONI

A VIEWER'S VIEWS

SAMPLES (2006), another performance piece, develops various aspects of ACTIONS IN NATURAL ENVIRONMENTS, but sets them in a gallery window, like a glass case. Huge titles announce the actions that are about to be performed.

VERY SMALL GROUP (2007), a workshop performance with a group of semi-amateurs, explores the notion of naming or belonging to very small groups.

An interactive installation, POINT OF VIEW (2007), takes a concept as its context, offers multiple points of view on apartments in a Swiss suburb.

With L'EFFET DE SERGE (2007), both a pun on "greenhouse effect" (*L'effet de "serre"*), and the exact description of the stage action, a string of special effects prepared by Serge for one or two friends each Sunday afternoon, the plot thickens, so to speak.

THE MELANCHOLY OF DRAGONS (2008) weaves back to the rock group in ITCHING, as a long-haired band, the Dragons, get stuck when their car breaks down on their way to opening an amusement park. The format evolves towards fable.

With BIG BANG (2010) the pattern blows up. On an ice field, a group of hairy prehistoric mammals play together. The title stops being descriptive, since the explosion it indicates might happen, unnoticed, between the first and the second parts. At this point, the action switches from a white downstage to backstage where the walls are painted green and the floor covered in water. Maybe the big bang has happened earlier, or maybe it hasn't yet. Hard to tell with this timeless theatre, and mystery sets in.

Many aspects of Quesne's theatre are contrasted in binary pairs: before/after, nature/culture, inside/outside, documentary/live action, downstage/upstage, stage right/stage left, effects/"natural" behaviours, white/green, real/unreal, instructions/chance. Filling in the gaps between these unexplained juxtapositions of contrasting elements is what stimulates and liberates the viewers' imaginations. But there is still more to this action, as Philippe Quesne's Vivarium Studio proceeds in an elegiac and surreal/hyperreal manner, slowly absorbing the audience into its saga.

[THE EXPERIENCE]

In a Vivarium Studio performance, there seems to be nothing more to see than what is shown. Performers "act natural," they keep their real names (except for Serge, played by Gaëtan Vourc'h, but that's for the sake of a pun). There is a dog, really named Hermes — the messenger of the gods. Props are recycled junk or novelty items. Performers cook, read or perform other everyday tasks. Elements of decor are conspicuously ersatz: a forest is made of branches taped on the floor; snow is wall-to-wall carpeting, fog is smoke produced by unhidden machines. In piece after piece — under their various avatars — the same tribe of normal-looking people appears, neither glamorous nor heroic.

The dialogues are minimal, non-existing or purposely non-audible and sometimes replaced by surtitles or silent movie title cards.

There is music. Somebody plays the guitar, or the recorder, to the obvious pleasure of the tribe sitting around the fire. Sometimes, unexpectedly, an outburst of well-known music highlights the absurdity of human endeavours by counterpointing a minute action, and the audience gets "beamed up" into **SUPERMAN**, **STAR WARS**, or Wagner's **WALKYRIE**. Otherwise, the atmosphere is quiet.

La Démangeaison des ailes
Photo © Philippe Quesne

A VIEWER'S VIEWS

The pace is slow. Because the eye sees faster than the action unravels, Quesne slows it down to make his point—"less is more" in a jungle of signs that nobody looks at anymore.

The action is factual. The premise of any work can be summed up in one or two sentences. Performers are dealing with one another only, not addressing the viewers.

Illusion returns—smoke, lights, spectacular music – but the methods of its making are undisguised, intended to be revealed, waltzing through popular imagery and collective memories.

It could be cinema, because the audience never seems to be taken into account—but it isn't. The screens have long been torn.

Each new work used to take up where the previous one had stopped, connected with a "link shot" of sorts: a man costumed as a bird ends ITCHING and opens DES EXPÉRIENCES which ends with scores of small tents that will open D'APRÈS NATURE; the astronauts' costumes ending D'APRÈS NATURE begin L'EFFET DE SERGE; dangling wigs ending SERGE appear very early on in THE MELANCHOLY OF DRAGONS. Today, it doesn't have to be as specific as a prop or costume, it can be a shared natural element. BIG BANG ends in water, which is central in BIVOUAC, the next episode on paper, but also in a site-specific experiment developed this summer in Bourgogne. This seems to point clearly to the progress of an unnamed saga.

Philippe Quesne pulls all the (invisible) strings during performances, and never stops developing an alphabet of signs, actions and tricks in-between stage productions. A visionary of the third kind is born: both a real-life storyteller and a serene conjurer.

Action en milieu naturel
Photo © Philippe Quesne

PHILIPPE QUESNE'S VIVARIUM STUDIO

[HAPPY FAMILIES]

Vivarium obviously belongs to a large family of theatre and image makers who, since the 1910s, have shattered narratives, characters, texts, sets, space…at a crossroad between visual, performing and performance arts.

To the expected historical medley — Duchamp, Dada, the Bauhaus, Surrealists, Gertrude Stein, Fluxus, Robert Wilson, or Richard Foreman — we could add cartoons, Hollywood, TV serials, serious literature and science-fiction. And John Cage. And Buster Keaton. Vivarium also belongs to a family with an eye on science, politics and the future of the planet.

His demiurge-like stance — is he a kid kicking in the ants' nest to stir things up in the performing arts, or a moralist of entomology, drawing what he observes with a microscope? — goes with a contrast between large scope and minute details, between the live and the represented.

Although there is an element of manipulation in Quesne's bewitching vision (which simultaneously shows you all the tricks), he does not belong to the family of ravishers, who impress their audiences emotionally with otherworldly or larger-than-life imagery. On the contrary, his manner of directing, both strict and open, fully enables the audience to free-associate with their own stack of references.

Funfairs and expos sound like areas worth exploring. Where else can you be photographed as a historical character by placing your head in a painted board; or watch a landscape unravel as if you were in movement, forgetting that behind the drop, somebody is laboriously turning a handle; or contemplate a **PANORAMA OF THE SWISS ALPS** reproduced in Paris at the end of the 19th century?

DENISE LUCCIONI

Going back in time, you could explore medieval mysteries performed in front of churches. But how about going deeper and having a look at the birth of proscenium stage theatre, coinciding with the invention of French gardens, both reflecting the universe and its cosmogony; or ancient Greek theatre, when theatres served outdoor re-enactments of the Pythia's prophecies in her secret temple?

Going into the future, biology, quantum physics and/or speculative realism also offer relevant avenues of research for personal readings and interpretations.

[LISTENING TO NATURE, AS PEOPLE OF THE FOREST OR THE ICE FIELD]

The development of a Vivarium work starts with conversations around a table, based on an idea, an image, a concept, or a link with the previous stage exploration. This first phase is likely to occur while the company is touring, which allows found elements and situations to be included. Imagine a group standing around the mouth of a geyser in Iceland, listening to its breath, just standing still and listening. And then transpose this type of non-action and presence to the stage.

[PHOTO GEYSER]

What is the sound of a single hand clapping?
Exactly.

Yet with Vivarium this is only the starting point. During rehearsals, the next phase, the work builds up. In the same way an artist paints, Quesne "uses" actors like touches of colour, giving them precise and very fast changing tasks to perform, indicating movements, positions, directions...No text yet. This may contradict an impression of spontaneity in performances. But by developing movement in time and space only—like a dance—Quesne orchestrates the performers, who later come up with their own words. Because composition in space and time and actions are right, because bodies move about "naturally," the words sound right.

Space and time—images and rhythms—are the materials that Philippe Quesne has to control in order to set up appropriate situations for "real" theatre to be born and magic to be performed.

[CECI N'EST PAS UNE PIPE]

With our view of the world arguably shaped by our mother tongue, Vivarium appeals to a common well of images and ideas by not using text, or by using it oddly. Quesne's vision does not need to be perceived intellectually or culturally.

Vivarium's saga is told in a "universal" language, because each viewer/hearer can identify individually with what is shown or uttered.

For instance, the local extras in **SERGE** colour the work differently whether in Finland, where the audience is reminded of Kaurismaki, or in Lisbon where Monteiro emerges in collective memory.

[PHOTO WALKYRIE]

It is also a matter of human scale and slow pace, that allow for togetherness here and now, watching and participating alike. Looking up at the signs on the walls of the cave.

And "time passes," as Serge says, the lowest common denominator between viewers and performers. Or perhaps the highest. Nature is as essential a connection: nature, meaning both the wilderness and human nature. Vivarium's work

DENISE LUCCIONI

A VIEWER'S VIEWS

apparently attempts to explore a primeval condition. Starting from scratch and rebuilding an environment. Starting from scratch and rebuilding a community. This is the tale patiently woven by Vivarium's saga.

Except for Icarus, whose appearance is more of an exorcism in ITCHING, things don't fall, they rise. While they occur in semi-darkness, there is always light glowing at a distance, *chiaroscuro*, a twilight zone. There is no underground, no weighing down of traditions, waters are shallow, ice is thin. Soaring out of dirt or water, tthey take the example of trees to find their way up. Getting out of caves to defeat shadows. Out of a junk of artefacts and conventions and castrating imagery, out of the mud of make-believes and artificial convictions. Vivarium's territory is the open air, actual or metaphorical. It is about climbing into the sky and light, looking at playful wonders, Serge's effects, the Dragons' numbers, a pile of inflatable boats.

[PHOTO ENCASED TREE]

Vivarium's pieces, born in a world repainted white, allow attempts at guessing what comes next in the saga, and lead into a future diving into other realities and dimensions, because it is theatre, because the viewers also participate, and the performers also watch other performers or viewers. And an obvious *mise en abîme* of image theatre comes to terms with a collective ritual, long lost, needing to be re-founded. As societies and political systems need to. Beyond rituals, primitive magic hovers.

[EPILOGUE]

The experience ends up operating as catharsis and building community spirit.

DENISE LUCCIONI

Together on a slow boat to China. Indicating a way for political action. Inventing one's life, rewriting one's reality. In tune.

Vivarium Studio is about "doing," "acting," bonding, one of the main reasons for theatre to exist. But Vivarium is also going back further in time, before theatre, before ritual, back to getting out of the cave, merging visions and projections, back to the magic of coming out into the light. A medium cyclically needs to reconsider its original purpose. At times, the struggle with gravity and darkness becomes a matter of life and death. Vivarium Studio does not only perform its double definition, it also acts out what its name announces. Alive, and live, through the fog. Showing a way for theatre and viewers alike. Out of the cave, time to get up and act.

And the **ALICE IN WONDERLAND** Cheshire cat comes to mind in a flash. Leaving its smile behind, like the trace of an experience, a message for the future, indelible and intangible, vital. A smile.

[PHOTO MAN/BIRD]

DENISE LUCCIONI

A VIEWER'S VIEWS

POSTSCRIPT

Magic: A primitive and neo-primitive practice aiming at influencing events and producing marvels.

DENISE LUCCIONI

MORE THAN A SYMPTOM: CURATING PERFORMING ARTS AS A JOB, CHALLENGE AND PURPOSE

FLORIAN MALZACHER

Among the professions that are rather close to art or even right within it, but that are not artistic themselves—not directly artistic themselves—the curator has the youngest and most unclear profile. In the visual arts, where he became a star within a short time, he is standing in the midst of a controversy that is essentially driven by himself. In the field of dance, theatre and performance however, he is still rare and, above all, mostly unheeded. Which is all the more surprising since he has long played an influential role in independent performing arts, defining and organizing art, discourses, formats and finances.

TERMINOLOGY AS SCARCE COMMODITY

The last 25 years, or so, have seen the strong development of a dance that explores the concept of choreography much further than ballet or even *Tanztheater* have dared, and a theatre that refuses to be defined by the borders of drama, of conventional divisions between performance and audience, of the imposed limitations of the genre. This independent and experimental international scene finds itself (together with its audiences) mostly outside of the fixed structures and relatively fixed aesthetics of the repertory city theatres, which are mainly active only within the limits of their own countries and languages. Just as unclear as the borders of this genre are many of the profiles of the jobs it has created or adapted: What does a dramaturg do without a drama, an art critic without a catalogue of criteria, a dancer without dance, a theatre director without a text that should be staged? The performing arts curator does not even have an outdated model of reference at his disposal: the terminology and job description have been borrowed from the visual arts, as their particular way of dealing with formats, with art and artists, and with economies and audiences, suddenly seemed to a certain degree transferable.

In the 1980s and early 1990s, a good part of the independent theatre landscape had changed considerably: radically new aestheticisms, and later new working structures and hierarchies within ensembles, collectives, and companies, came into existence along with new or newly defined theatre houses such as Mickery in Amsterdam, Kaaitheater in Brussels, de Single in Antwerp, Hebbel-Theater in Berlin, TAT (Theater am Turm) in Frankfurt, Teatergarasjen in Bergen, Ménagerie de verre in Paris and many more. Additionally, festivals such as Eurokaz in Zagreb, Inteatro in Polverigi, Festival d'Automne in Paris and later KunstenfestivalDesArts in Brussels, as well as the professional network IETM, offered new possibilities for a dense international exchange. Above all, the concept of the Belgium *kunstencentra* such as Vooruit in Gent or Stuk in Leuven (which, with their open, mostly interdisciplinary approaches, replaced conventional ensemble theatres and paved the way for many of today's scene-heroes and re-classified audiences) has spilled over into neighbouring countries and made it possible to reinvent theatre as an institution.

With them arrived a new, often charismatically filled professional profile: that of the programme maker (who, depending on the institution, would be officially called Artistic Director, *Intendant*, dramaturg, manager, producer). As the name already shows, the accent was on taking a grip on things, on making. A generation of men of action defined the course of events — and even if their attitude seems occasionally patriarchal from today's point of view, the scene was actually less male-biased than the society and the city theatres around it. This generation of founders, which at the same time redefined and imported the model of the dramaturg, established some remarkably efficient and stabile structures and publics: it was a time of invention and discovery, which has had obvious repercussions into the present day. Professional profiles were created and changed — including that of the artist. This foundation work was largely completed by the mid-1990s at the latest (at least in the West), not least because financial resources were becoming more scarce. What followed was a generation of former assistants, of critical apprentices so to say, and with them a period of continuity, but also of differentiation, reflection, and well-tailored networks, of development and re-questioning new formats—labs and residencies, summer academies, *parcours*, thematic mini-festivals, emerging artist platforms... The difficulty of the plains replaces that of the mountains, the struggle over quality criteria and discourses replaces the often socio-cultural founding-impetus to let very different cultures coexist equally.

The picture is still dominated by transition models, but the strong specialisation of the arts (exemplified by the visual arts), the subsequent specialisation of the programme makers and dramaturgs, and a generally altered professional world—which also here increasingly relies on free, independent, as well as cheaper labour—along with increasingly differentiated audiences, again require a different professional profile: the curator is a symptom of these changes in art, as well as in society and the market. His working fields are theatre forms that often cannot be realised within the established structures; artistic handwritings that always require different approaches; a scene that is more and more internationalised and disparate; the communication of often difficult aestheticisms; transmission and contextualisation. Last but not least, the curator is the link between art and the public.

Whether the stolen term "curator" is the most suitable here for this job or not is currently a popular point of dispute and, above all, polemics. However, there is more at stake than personal gain in distinction to programme makers, who might not feel appreciated enough. And the difficulty of naming and defining this new job is just symptomatic for a genre in which terminology is a scarce commodity anyway and which does not even have a reasonably good name itself: Experimental theatre? Free theatre? All biased or misleading. Time-based art? Live art? At least attempts at defining the genres within different borders. Devised theatre, that is, a theatre that must evolve again and again from scratch? New theatre—after all these years? Postdramatic theatre? At least one successful, marketable keyword. But how does the kind of dance that has been so influential in recent years, but is also still looking for a suitable name, fit in here: conceptual dance?

As a clandestine romantic, one might consider the missing slate to be a subversive gain—an elitist thinking in niches, but out of defensive resignation rather than self-confidence. In fact, the lack of terminology indicates above all a lack of articulation, a lack of communication not limited to advertising, a lack of more than purely intra-disciplinary discourse in the performing arts, which remain amazingly speechless in this respect. Thus it again signals the necessity of curatorial work, which—as can be seen in the visual arts, where catalogues, for example, are an integral part of almost all exhibitions—consists to a large extent of verbalisation, communication and discussion. As a part of the central task to create contexts.

CONCRETE CONTEXTS

Contexts. Links between artists, artworks, audiences, cultures, social and political realities, parallel worlds, discourses, institutions. It is not by chance that the curator in the visual arts sphere emerged at a time when artworks often no longer functioned without a context, *refused* to function without a context. When they on the contrary began to define themselves precisely through their contexts, when they began to search or even create them, and to critically question the institutions that surrounded them. When the idea of an auratic artwork and auratic author disappeared and was replaced by art that was no longer understandable without relations. Additionally, the amount of information about and from our world and the complexity of art has risen exponentially—as has the amount of art produced. The curator was both a cause and a result of this development.

Thus, the frequently expressed wish of artists in the fields of dance and theatre (more seldom expressed in the visual arts) that their work be presented unexplained and un-contextualised, standing alone, without a framework, moves along the thin line between justified fear of reduction, simplification and domestication on the one side, and the misjudgement of the ways their work functions on the other. The muteness of the genre extends to all those who participate in it.

Thus, good curatorial work would consist not in damaging the autonomous artwork in its autonomy, but on the contrary, in reinforcing it, yet without considering it untouchable, too weak, needy of protection. How near should the framework get to the artwork, how closely should one be juxtaposed to the other, how charged should the surrounding be: these are central points of discussion between artists and curators in exhibition art—but they are just as valid when making programmes for a festival or a theatre house. Contexts can offer artworks a proper reception—but they can also incapacitate them.

And yet, theatre and dance performances are not paintings, transportable artefacts, or even clearly defined installations. Few exhibitions have the complexity and unpredictability of a festival. As a social form of art, theatre will always have a different attitude towards pragmatism and compromise, will need more time and space, and therefore stay inferior to other genres regarding agility. In an age of speed and spacelessness that might be a market flaw, just as it was an advantage in other times. But however cumbersome and relatively small the possibilities of contextualisation may be within a festival or a season condensed to knots, they can also be very effective. The fact of not-being-able-to-control is a challenge that must be faced in a productive way, since not-wanting-to-control in this case only produces boredom.

So what can one see if one attends, on one evening, two clearly juxtaposed performances? How does it change one work retrospectively and the other in advance? (At least an exhibition curator rarely has the possibility of steering the order of reception so precisely). What influence does it exert on the reception if a *leitmotif* or a theme is offered as the focus? What reference points can be given for an artwork—perhaps also historically, at least on paper or video? What contexts of experience are created for the spectators already by the very choice of space, the point of time, the graphic design, the advertising strategies? Is it possible not only to scatter theoretical postulates like parsley over the programme, but also actually mix them in?

These are only some arbitrary examples of how contexts and focuses can be created—generally through the elaboration of smaller sections or agglomerations/knots in the programme as a whole. After all, biennials and museums are rarely adroit ships either—and yet they increasingly play with their temporal axis, with the idea of the performative, the social. The fact that the figure of the exhibition maker—for example, a new type of curator such as Harald Szeeman—became so important in the 1970s is due not least to the fact that the exhibition increasingly became a happening itself, bordered or permeated by accompanying events, occasionally changing, understanding itself within time. Szeemann compared his work quite early to that of a theatre director. In the 1990s,

The Game with Objects curated by
Florian Malzacher — Photo: Petra Zanki

art was frequently adopting the definition of the exhibition framework and discovering itself as a social space: Nicolas Bourriaud has termed it "relational aesthetics" and Maria Lind speaks of "performative curating." It is hardly possible to penetrate more deeply into the neglected core business of the theatre.

So this attention towards an arc, towards a dramaturgy of programming, is also an attempt at recovering lost terrain for theatre as a form of art. A course of events, a change of tempo, a change of intensity, a change of viewpoint. Even if barely any spectator can follow such dramaturgies in their entirety, they are nevertheless perceptible. One can walk through a festival as through a landscape. Some things are accidental, others are obvious. To linger or to go on, to grasp things intuitively or turn them over intellectually. The phantom of the *über*-curator, boldly creating his own piece out of other people's artworks, is not to be feared in the performative domain anyway. On the contrary, there is rather a lack of courage for imparting meaning at all—and not least because of modesty, but out of fear of the task.

Local context plays a role here more than in other arts; even the rather small audience that is interested in advanced forms of theatre is far less informed about the actual art field as a whole than its counterparts in the visual arts, film or music: it travels less and its artworks are more difficult to access, respectively not reproducible in catalogues. As a rule (except for a few big cities), it is a single venue or a single festival that alone defines the horizon of the audience (as well as that of the local professional critics). The terrain of its judgement is paradoxically demarcated by the curator himself—only the art that he is showing actually exists. Thus, international artworks are forcedly localised and placed into relation to that which is familiar. The state of the art is different in each town.

CRITERIA AND COMPROMISES

Whether locally or internationally, in the end it's clear: it's all about choice, about defining who is allowed to be a part of it, allowed to produce and present, allowed to earn money. Programme makers have a function in the art market and however much their opinions may differ, together they delineate the limited field. Who they don't see, who they refuse to see, has — at least internationally — almost no chance of being seen. At the same time, never before has so much art been produced, nor so many artists emerged. While the budgets shrink, more and more schools, Master's programmes, university departments are being founded, producing more and more artists, mostly without considering what this overproduction may produce in itself. In terms of market, of quality, but also with regards to the personal situations of the former students, who are often not needed, not wanted and (too often) simply not good enough to survive in the highly competitive market. The task of organising this field, the task of playing the bad guy, has been delegated: curating means excluding and this excluding has existential consequences for artists.

So what are the criteria for such a selection? Yes, of course: good art, bad art. What we consider as such. Defined by education, experience, taste. By opinion. By the discourses we believe in. They are difficult to name, these criteria, and they consist of various aspects. It obviously is a thin line indeed between dogmatism and arbitrariness. It defines itself through a clear style, a recognisable handwriting perhaps, through coherency of the programme, through a dramaturgy of procedure, through relationships. Through stringency. Of course it's true: just as most city theatres put together their programme out of all kinds of art for all kinds of audiences, thus also most international festivals and venues are just as well marked by a difficult-to-discern mixture of conviction and pragmatism.

The arguments for keeping it somewhat broader are numerous and all programme makers are schooled in them: not excluding any segment of the public, creating contexts, setting more audacious pieces aside for more popular ones, visitor numbers, ticket sales, tolerance towards other artistic approaches, financial difficulties and more. Indeed, it doesn't help anyone if a curator primarily wants to prove his own courage with his programme for—eventually at the cost of the artists. To establish and maintain a festival, to bind an audience, to win allies, and thus to create a framework also for artworks that are more consequential, more audacious, and more cumbersome is important. Especially since free spaces for art are becoming fewer and fewer, since the struggle of all programme makers for the survival of their programmes is becoming tougher and tougher.

And yet, what is the use of maintaining for something if it is no longer visible? If it is no longer legible, what is necessary and compellable in the midst of the pragmatic? The model of the curator is also a counter-model of the cultural manager, who values many things, who stakes off a broad field of creative and artistic activities, whose aim is, after all, socio-cultural. Curatorial work also means deciding clearly for oneself what is good and what is bad. And knowing why.

But a good programme does not consist simply or necessarily only of good performances. On the one side, the decision in favour of co-productions and against merely bought-in guest performances is immensely important in terms of cultural policy. But it is also a decision for risk, the results imponderable; the right decisions can lead to a bad festival if one reads it only with respect to its results rather than its endeavours. On the other side, it is about creating internal relationships—even if a festival does not give itself a thematic red thread. Whether a programme is well thought out depends on the combination of different formats, aestheticisms and arguments within a nevertheless very clearly outlined profile. But it also depends on the supposedly more pragmatic, but often no less dramaturgical considerations, which can play a considerable role in the beauty of a programme: for it can indeed happen that a performance is simply too long for a particular slot. Or too short. Or needs a different sort of stage. That it is the wrong genre. Thematically or aesthetically too similar to another show. Or too different. And yet, if it is worth it, one will probably find a solution. And yes, one must also fill in the slots: young, entertaining, political, conceptual, new, established…But there is also this: as soon as one stumbles across a piece that one wants to present by all means, one will quickly forget about this basic structure. If one is left with some spare money, of course.

Moreover, the local question belongs to the list of possible criteria: what possibilities are there for changing or influencing the scene of a town in terms of infrastructure—but also for presenting it, for giving it visibility and capacity for confrontation and growth. Every curator will say: one must primarily think in terms of quality. And yet, consciously or not, he will measure with a double standard. There is a thin line here as well: without local and also sustainable effects, an internationally oriented theatre house or festival will largely remain without impact and without backing in hard times. And vice versa: even the finest motives can soon turn into provinciality and lack of significance beyond the region.

While artistic work survives through consistency and the greatest possible resistance to compromise, a festival programme, a seasonal programme, even a small *parcours*, will always carry compromise within it like a birthmark. It is also for this reason that the curator is not an artist. This discrepancy is essential and often painfully indelible. Not only because curators are often too ready for concessions. And not only because artists rarely make good curators: their view is always either to narrow (since they are guided by their own aesthetic intransigence) or too broad (since they are guided by social and solidary thoughts and feelings).

There is no reason why compromise should be romanticised with heroic pathos of action ("The show must go on"). But it will always remain a subject of conflict—especially where the art itself is existential, radical, ready to take risks. The quest of the absolute will bump against the necessity of presenting a turnkey product in the end. All the new modules of processual work, all those labs and residencies, are merely vents that eventually miss the real problem: it is not about not being willing to finish, being able to finish. It is that "finished" should be defined differently for each project.

WHAT MARKET?

As a programme maker, one relegates a part of the constraints one is unable to absorb to the artists. So, where is the limit? How long should one fight, when should one give up? How long is it good to preserve something, even if reduced, and when is it better to withdraw? What is hasty obedience to politics and money? And what is litigant quixotism?

The market of independent theatre, and eventually theatre as such, is a well-cushioned one, mostly regulated through public money and foundations. In recent times, more and more sponsors have come into play, but in Europe their role is still mostly too limited to have an influence on the programme that would be worth mentioning: the fact that the Dublin Fringe Festival recently—since the emergence of a vodka producer as its main sponsor—changed its name into Absolut Fringe is still an unusual case, perhaps heralding the future. Mostly the market is too small, the audience too marginal, the profit too limited, and the genre not sexy enough for big time investors. Also the volatile medium is rather unsuitable for the free art market: a performance cannot be bought and hung on a wall; it cannot be collected and doesn't gain value; it does not even impart a special status. That is why the artists of performance art (to be distinguished from the performing arts) have have taken much care since the 1970s, together with their galleries, to ensure that the supposedly ephemeral aspect of their work should not be to their financial disadvantage—and have elevated video or photo documentation to the status of artefacts. A live art is performance art only for the brief moment before the immaterial work has clotted into an object. Theatre and dance makers, however, have almost no access to this kind of free market, to that form of old age insurance. Which at least has the advantage that a curator (or art critic) cannot profit from the artworks of those artists whom he is promoting—we are spared this potential corruption.

On the other hand, many a visual artist will cast a look of envy to the subvention market of dance and theatre, since it seems to offer protection against the sometimes hysterical capitalism of the free art market. But the 80s are long gone: the subventions, sinking anyway, are increasingly spent on the maintenance of institutions that are weighty in real estate and personnel, and little is left for the slim independent scene. Whereas Western European countries can mostly still nibble at the achievements from the previous years, countries that could not knot an infrastructural security network are mostly left to the direct mercy of economy with its ups and downs.

Surely there is an individual market value in theatre as well, surely it is important, of course, at which festival or in which venue one can be seen. But the demand regulates the price only to a certain degree, and the system of salaries remains comparably limited. Thus, the pressure of the market can only climb so high—but it does not diminish for the artists, who have mostly precarious existences, and not just when they are beginning their careers. In the eyes of many artists, the curator, the programme maker, the director is — despite all amiability — part of a system of humiliation, which remains obscure, since its criteria are insufficiently reflected both by the curators and by the artists. Austrian writer Thomas Bernhard once wrote to his publisher Siegfried Unseld that the main problem was that each publisher had many authors, but each author had only one publisher. A theatre maker may have more than one producer — yet the unequal relationship of dependence, both economic and psychological, remains similar.

But obviously the programme makers are not independent either. The money that they distribute, or maybe invest, is obtained from their employers, mostly political ones (who again have it via taxes from the people). They are rarely subjected to direct thematic pressure towards making specific programmes, at least in the West; politics and the public usually no longer exert their influence with regard to a specific type of art and a specific discourse — barely anyone wants to be denounced as a conservative ignorant. Instead, the course is already set before the appointment or through the appointment of the artistic direction, then the discussion is usually reduced to economic factors, cost-effectiveness, sustainability and capacity utilisation rather than to themes and aestheticisms. Since festivals and theatre houses are never cost efficient, they should at least be profitable on the other side: through urban marketing, image, tourism, number of overnight stays…And yet, engaging in an argument of indirect returns via Richard Florida's rhetoric of the "creative class" is dangerous for art institutions — on the one hand, the reduction of art to numbers can hardly be reversed, and on the other hand, economic arguments are often just pretextual, behind them stands the same old doubt as to the necessity of contemporary art, whose value has drastically sunken with the disappearance of the once mocked *Bildungsbürger* from politics.

Programme makers are indeed responsible for the money with which they have been entrusted. Contractually, they are usually answerable to their public funders (at least indirectly, through politically appointed supervisory boards). And morally? To the artists? The art? The audience? The dilemma is intensified through the fact that there is, unlike in the world of museums, only rarely any difference between a director and a curator—and freelance curators with independence and autonomy are even more scarce. Thus, the political pressure of numbers is exerted directly on the person that creates the programme—mixed loyalties are unavoidable. The model of the curator is therefore decisively not that of a director; he is supposed to be responsible primarily to artists, art, specific discourses and specific aestheticisms. An imaginary (perhaps naïve) figure rather than a reality. A construct, at least.

THE STARBUCKS COFFEE OF ART

But perhaps the problem lies not so much in the fact that there is inequality, that there is injustice, that there is always a hidden agenda behind the association of curators and artists, or that their relationship is always also an economic one. Perhaps the problem resides much more in the fact that it is precisely the theatre, that large machine for reflecting the world and oneself, that lacks sufficient reflection on the mechanisms to which we, the programme makers, curators, artistic directors, are exposed, mechanisms that we, however, also use and sometimes generate ourselves. That we tend to console ourselves quickly with the belief that without us it would all be even worse, that we are still taking the best out of a situation that is becoming worse.

We are products of what Slavoj Žižek has termed "cultural capitalism:" we drink the Starbucks coffee of art and we are happy that a part of our money protects the rainforest (for example: conceptual dance, young artists, research). It is a

The Game with Objects curated by Per Ananiassen — Photo: Petra Zanki pseudo-proper action, since eventually it primarily protects the system whose spikes we believe to be filing down. It is the same system in which we first produce the defects and then we try to alleviate them. We want power that should not be recognisable as such.

Thus, barely anything that the profession of the curator in the performing arts consists of is new in itself. And yet, it is important to see how the professional image differs from other genres, as well as from the programme maker of the founders' generation. From that of the production dramaturg. From that of the intendant, the artistic director, the manager. The independent performing arts, these arts in a niche without a proper name, need articulation, contextualisation, discourses and publicity in order to be able to take their deserved place among the contemporary arts. The curator is one of the symptoms of a change. Seen that way, it is indeed a gain in distinction. But less so for the ones who call themselves curators than for an art form that should be finally recognised as more than an exotic accessory to city theatres and repertory companies.

> This text is a revised version of a text published in Frakcija #55 "Curating Perfoming Arts". The translation is based on the translation by Marina Miladinov.

MORE THAN A SYMPTOM

FLORIAN MALZACHER

ESSAY 6

POSITIVE ACTS: THE EVOLUTION OF PAN PAN THEATRE COMPANY

NOELIA RUIZ

INTRODUCTION

When Pan Pan Theatre was formed, in 1991, the theatrical landscape in Ireland was primarily dominated by the Western form *par excellence*: the dramatic text. Apart from Operating Theatre, created as a contemporary music-theatre company in 1980 by Olwen Fouéré and Roger Doyle, the experimental performance scene had little representation on Irish soil.

Ireland had produced many outstanding playwrights, but outside the dramatic frame there were very few companies devising original work. And even then, the general inclination was towards physical theatre in its different forms, as it was the case of the works of Tom McIntyre in the 80s, Sligo's Blue Raincoat Theatre Company, formed in 1991, and companies such as Barabbas or Loose Canon created later in the nineties. But there were no precedents in Irish theatre of a company led by conceptual art.

According to Gavin Quinn, co-founder and co-artistic director of Pan Pan, there was a reason why this type of work had not been prolific in the country.

> Well, there was never an avant-garde in Ireland because we were quite small, we weren't industrialised, we missed industrialisation and therefore the slow development of the economy, and the slow development of other aspects of society led to conservatism and parochialism. So our path was quite different than other European countries and all the great Irish artist tended to do it by exile, sort of create in exile.

The initial drive behind the company was the desire to create theatre more in tune with continental European aesthetics.

> We started Pan Pan because we weren't really interested in any theatre that was being made in Dublin at the time. We were just interested in starting a company that would make

The Rehearsal, Playing The Dane Photo: Ros Kavanagh

theatre like the French model of theatre art, as opposed to the craft of making theatre, which was prevalent at the time. So the company started to explore those ideas of a more European aesthetic and the simple idea of theatre being conceptual, and very much a medium where you could use the kind of visual arts principles of line, form, colour. And that was the reason why it began.

Apart from the avant-garde, Quinn acknowledges specific inspiration from the Cartel, a group created in 1927 by Parisian directors Louis Jouvet, Charles Dullin, Gaston Baty and Georges Pitoëf with the aim of renovating the theatre scene, particularly reacting against commercial theatre and what they called "théâtre de boulevard".

There was this idea of conceptual theatre, of theatre being free, theatre being whatever it needs to be, theatre being idiosyncratic and very much an art form as against just a craft, because the complication of theatre has always been this need to sell tickets and its success is seen through the number of audience that go and see it.

Indeed, making this type of work in Ireland in the early nineties was courageous and hardly box-office oriented. For Quinn, though, it is the responsibility of theatre makers to create work outside established parameters:

Generally speaking the people who make theatre are probably more conservative than the audience — it's not the other way around, as people would necessarily think. If it isn't there to look at — if the environment is not there — it is very hard for [audiences] to appreciate.

Quinn might have a point. Since he founded the company with designer Aedín Cosgrove, as graduates from Trinity College Dublin, they have created 23 theatre and performance pieces, toured their work worldwide, and received multiple national and international awards.

Playboy of the Western World
Photo: Ros Kavanagh

The symbiosis between director and designer produced an experimental theatre company without precedent in Ireland, and it has been precisely this lack of precedent that has freed them to establish their own.

Pan Pan's experimental drive insists on a constant evolution and the company's projects vary immensely in form, content and approach. Thus, some of their shows are adaptations of—or, more accurately, "responses" to—classical dramatic texts such as **MACBETH** (which they interpreted as **MAC-BETH 7** (in 2004) or **HAMLET** (staged as **THE REHEARSAL, PLAYING THE DANE** in 2010); or canonical material like the myth of Oedipus (**OEDIPUS LOVES YOU**, 2006) co-written by Simon Doyle and Gavin Quinn, which initially was conceived as a collection of songs with sound designer Jimmy Eadie.

Other works are original shows created in collaboration with different artists, such as **ONE: HEALING WITH THEATRE**, which started as a photographic project, evolved into a documentary film and finally became a performance/installation piece. These have been hallmarks of a company that seeks new challenges, taking risks in a constant investigation of theatre and possible languages of performance. It is how Pan Pan has developed its own signature.

FROM NEGATIVE ACT TO PAN PAN INTERNATIONAL THEATRE SYMPOSIUM

Pan Pan's fascination with the avant-garde was conspicuous from their first production, **NEGATIVE ACT**, written and directed by Gavin Quinn, which was premiered in the Lombard Street Studio Theatre (now Green On Red Galleries) and performed later that year in Lyon International Student Festival, France. It was inspired by **THE FUTURIST SYNTHETIC THEATRE MANIFESTO** by F. T. Marinetti, Emilio Settimelli and Bruno Colla (1915), an idiosyncratic treatise that urged succinctness in time, word and action, broke with Aristotelian unities and most other theatrical conventions, and stressed the reality-blurring qualities of theatricality.

The search for theatricality—its essential quality that makes it different to any other art form—had started during late 19th century modernism, when Adolphe Appia developed his ideas on scenography, space and the human body, but more specifically in the use of lighting. Along with Edward Gordon Craig, they were very influential for the next generation of theatre makers who explored similar concepts, understanding the stage as a site of sensual exploration, aiming to create an atmosphere through action, words, line, colour and rhythm.[1] Craig's idea of the *Über-Marionette*, or the ideal actor, highlighted the actor's presence as the "producer of theatricality and the channel through which it passes"[2] to the audience.

NEGATIVE ACT, says Quinn,

> was a very abstract notion of four characters, in which one kept writing away from the other three. The title comes from the notion of doing nothing, the idea of nothingness, so the play itself was about nothing. Just using time onstage and being very much about building a language from nothing.

The avant-garde influence was also present in the company's next two productions, THE CRYSTAL SPIDER, written by the French pioneer of anti-realistic drama Madame Rachilde in 1892, and THE MAN WITH TWO KISSES, based on the play by the Polish avant-garde playwright Stanislaw Witkiewicz, THE MADMAN AND THE NUN, written in 1922.

Both productions would further define Pan Pan's trajectory. Witkiewicz came from a visual arts background, and his main aim was to create thematic abstractions onstage by dismissing conventional form. His dissertation *An Introduction* to the Theory of Pure Form in the Theatre* is a testimony of the avant-garde rebellion against psychological realism. In general, Witkiewicz plays seem to distil an unreasonable logic with the aim of creating a distance from any concrete association with reality. These traits would also go on to become a feature of Pan Pan's aesthetics, not only in terms of form, but also thematically and with regards to acting style.

> These two performances were looking pretty much at the early 20th century experimental writing, especially writing for the theatre that was linked to literary movements and visual arts movements, symbolism and, I suppose, expressionism. Symbolist drama is essentially about creating a unique atmosphere, which isn't necessarily surreal or real, and very much about connecting time, obviously theatre being classically a time-based art. We also focused a lot on talking to an audience directly, not in a Brechtian way but just actually communicating to an audience, to that moment when they wish to watch.

Their next play, **MARTIN ASSASSIN OF HIS WIFE. A DEAF OPERA FOR THEATRE**, premiered in Project Arts Centre in 1994 and went to The Everyman Theatre in Liverpool. It was the first of a few collaborations with other writers. In 1995 Pan Pan created **A BRONZE TWIST OF YOUR SERPENT MUSCLES** for the Brouhaha International Arts Festival in Liverpool, which was awarded Best Overall Production in the first Dublin Theatre Fringe Festival, and was also presented in Imaginaire Irlandais Festival, La Friche de Belle Mai, Marseille, France in 1996. It was described as "A study of decay, madness, erotic perversion and complex psychopathic personalities told through mime, dance and music."[3]

Thematically there was already a pattern growing in which the darkest and most solitary places of the mind and its consequent social and personal dysfunctions are manifested in chimerical environments. This became allied to another trait: the use of live music on stage, which in this instance was played by the band The Idiots.

In only three years Pan Pan had created a name for themselves, and packed houses reflected a thirst for such innovative theatre pieces. The company not only defied dramatic form, but any labelling. Their shows were made more identifiable by an eerie visual language in which images were constantly altered, at times frantically, along with the estrangement of silence. Their next show, TAILORS REQUIEM, premiered at the L'Imaginaire Irlandais Festival France in 1996, and was subsequently presented in Project Arts Centre during the Dublin Theatre Festival, the Edinburgh Festival Fringe, Spectrum Festival Austria and Riksteatern Festival Stockholm, Sweden.

Touring around continental Europe not only had an influence on their own practice, it also encouraged Quinn and Cosgrove to bring their new discoveries home, and, in 1997 they produced and directed The Pan Pan International Theatre Symposium, which took place initially biennially and then annually until 2003. It was driven by a will to show contemporary groundbreaking work that didn't reach Irish stages. "We just decided we'd make an idealistic festival, since we started off as an idealistic company," says Quinn,

> so we brought five or six companies for the whole week where they could perform, watch other performances, and attend workshops and other kinds of engagements, having engaged discussions about theatre, and ask the question which Brecht said every generation has to ask, the question of what theatre is. Then it developed into a much bigger festival until finally we produced something like eight performances from all kinds of companies from around the world. We combined old companies and new companies, so we would have actors from Théâtre du Soleil and Big Art Group from New York, La Carnicería from Madrid, or Última Vez from Belgium. This combination of old and new was interesting. And then we

would try to mix the Irish companies in with all that, sometimes commissioning them to make new work, sometimes interacting with the international companies. It became a very interesting, sort of well-attended, very rich week. It became so big, though, that we decided we'd better park it because it's good when something is very successful just to end it. Our plan is perhaps in some way in the future to sort of re-ignite it again. It's very interesting for theatre artists to create festivals, as against them all being created by large institutions or, let's say, producers.

The type of work showed during the symposia was mostly in line with contemporary European theatre aesthetics as developed since the 70s, which have been recently labelled as postdramatic theatre by Hans-Thies Lehmann.[4] Lehmann understands postdramatic as a theatre that 'is confronted with the questions of possibilities beyond drama'. The term is closely related to the postmodern stance. In the arts this stance is manifested in certain traits like collage, montage, parody, irony, juxtaposition, self-reflexivity, and the overlay of popular culture and high cultural references, which is often manifested in a mix of styles, and a reflection on intertextuality. Any modernist master narrative or teleology is nullified, together with any certainties, and a new relativism and cynicism permeates the postmodern standpoint. In theatre and performance the abandonment of traditional dramatic structure is an analogy to the rejections of those master narratives in favour of disjointed ones. Many of these characteristics are very palpable in postdramatic work, along with a focus on audience experience versus passive observation, highlighting the liveness of performance: the unique and unrepeatable encounter between audience and performers.

This type of work would have an impact on the evolution of Pan Pan's aesthetics. For instance, in the early 2000s there was a proliferation of technological devices within contemporary theatre, especially the use of live video and projections, which was prominent in much of the work shown in Pan Pan's last Symposium. The use of technology reinforced disjointed and simultaneous actions onstage, pointing at interrupted but concurrent narratives. The performance mode defied the idea of "character" in favour of the performer's presence and unaffected delivery, leaving no room for any dramatic artifice.

In Pan Pan's MAC-BETH 7, which premiered in Project Arts Centre in 2004, these traits are abundant, and some of them would recursively appear in future productions. Live projections took place on TV screens aligned in a column, featuring different pages of the script—some of those covered in worms—which were manipulated live by highlighting some of the lines, scribbling, or covering them with dead flowers. Onstage and background actions were also projected simultaneously, along with other images related to the central topic of greed and the seven deadly sins.

The set design allowed for a multiplicity of meanings, complementing the fragmented performance text, in which a standard secondary-school analysis of the play was included, representing the MACBETH known to the majority of an Irish audience through the Leaving Certificate State examination. This intertextual and self-referential device would also become a feature in Pan Pan's work. To reinforce the point, the set had the air of a classroom, with school desks at both sides of the stage and with the actors dressing as secondary school students with a playground seesaw centre stage to enforce the point. Upstage, a long booth made of fibreglass subverted the idea of privacy, perhaps pointing to the tenets of reality TV in which the personal is made public.

The seven performers alternated between roles, this being signified by change of costume and scenic action. The exception was an eight-year-old girl who played Hecate, the queen of witches. The use of a variety of styles included opera, which served to deliver some of the most heightened moments in the play, adding to the disengaged performance mode that since MAC-BETH 7 has become a trademark of Pan Pan, and which was probably influenced by Quinn's direction of Mozart's opera THE MAGIC FLUTE in 2002, which was nominated for Best Opera Production in The Irish Times Theatre Awards.

MAC-BETH 7 was very well received in Ireland and abroad, marking a highpoint in the trajectory of Pan Pan and consolidating their aesthetics as a company.

PAN PAN'S AESTHETICS: PERFORMANCE STYLE, SCENOGRAPHY AND THEMES

Although Pan Pan is in constant evolution and their projects vary immensely in form, content and approach, they are all driven by the two basic principles of audience experience and a manifest conception of a specific atmosphere. This is achieved by their mise-en-scène and performance/acting mode. Like Richard Maxwell and the New York City Players, Pan Pan has developed a unique style in terms of the quality Quinn seeks in actors, and in this sense it has been compared by Ben Brantley in The New York Times to Lars von Triers: "a largely affectless acting style that recalls the Dogme school of film."[5]

"Well, it's very particular," Quinn says of Pan Pan's acting style.

> I have worked with actors for a long time and you are looking at what's interesting. For some actors it's their personality. For others it's the personality plus the way they act. For others it's just developing a notion. Acting evolves and it becomes more contemporary, trying to get reality into acting, which is not about being naturalistic or about being symbolic or about classic acting, it's getting liveness into acting and releasing something from the performer. So it's really a mixture of the idea of presence, and the idea of personality and the idea

Oedipus Loves You — Photo: Ros Kavanagh

of theatre in itself: how people can objectify and get outside themselves. I think it's also about making them want to be on stage, not just pretending to be onstage or lying when they are on stage or hiding the fact that they are onstage. There is really no one way of describing it. Some of the actors think that it is just that I don't want them to act, but that's not true, because they are acting anyway.

Many contemporary theatre makers use the word "task" to describe how actions onstage should be addressed with a spontaneity that seeks the quality of improvisation or unpredictability to achieve realness as opposed to rehearsed repetition. Quinn's approach draws from the idea of task but he takes a step further in demanding from the actors a connection with the audience, bringing the spectators into the world of the play. This is done through direct address and by treating the spectator as an accomplice by means of exchanged glances, for example, encouraging them to decide what the performers are actually thinking. Thus, dialogues get filtered through the audience, through the acknowledgement that it is their perception that ultimately gives meaning to the situation at hand.

This dramaturgical strategy is explained by Lehmann as turning "the level of the real explicitly into a 'co-player,'" with the aim of producing a certain "indecidability" between reality and fiction.[6] For Lehmann, "the aesthetic distance of the spectator is a phenomenon of dramatic theatre; in the new forms of theatre that are closer to performance this distance is structurally shaken."[7]

"We've always focused on the audience," says Quinn, "how we can be clear to an audience, how we can establish and re-establish that contact, and how we can have this really good atmosphere between the audience and this interesting exchange of energy. It's all about completion, to be completed by the audience." Lehmann categorises this approach

Mac-Beth 7 – Photo: Ros Kavanagh

as "the production of situations for the *self-interrogation, self-exploration, self-awareness* of all participants. […] a re-version of the artistic act towards the viewers takes place."[8]

The visual style of Pan Pan seems to subscribe to postdramatic aesthetics as well. The underlying concept is the design of a world, not according to symmetrical structuring and logic but rather to a metonymic use of space:

> we can call a scenic space metonymic if it is not primarily defined as symbolically standing in for another fictive world but is instead highlighted as part and continuation of the real theatre space.[9]

This spatial dramaturgy is possible by the combination of scenography and performing practice, which work symbiotically and become—like the audience—a co-player. This was specifically played with in **THE REHEARSAL, PLAYING THE DANE** where from the very beginning the division between audience and performers is rescinded. To start with, a rehearsed reading of the text takes place, and a member of the audience is asked at random to read one of the characters. Next, the audience is confronted with an audition for the character of Hamlet—which is a reflection on all the possible Hamlets scholarly research and theatre productions have portrayed—with Quinn and his team onstage auditioning the possible candidates (there are three). The actors not only performed as if it was a real audition, but also talked about their real relationship with the play and the main character, stereotypically one of the most coveted parts by male actors. Subsequently, the spectators were asked to cast the Hamlet that would play the part for the rest of the show, by making them walk onstage and stand next to the actor they preferred. The boundaries between real and fictional spaces where blurred and the audience was made responsible for—or at least self-aware-of their choices, feeling perhaps the sense of success or failure actors go through when they get or do not get a part. Most of Pan Pan's productions achieve a similar effect by acknowledging the place the audience and performers inhabit: a performance space. To emphasise this, the visual dramaturgy is often purposely flawed, allowing for the lack of concealment on stage in which the actors change costumes, manipulate lighting—as in THE CRUMB TRAIL which featured overhead projectors—or other devices—such as smoke machines in THE REHEARSAL, PLAYING THE DANE—openly exposing the theatrical tricks, or "the triumph of theatricality over illusionism."[10] This is further enhanced by the use of elements such as props that are sometimes random, other times semiotic and, like an ideogram, express the idea of something without referring to it directly. Similarly to MAC-BETH 7, in THE REHEARSAL, PLAYING THE DANE Victorian ruffs and candles were sufficient to suggest an epoch, co-existing with oversized metallic bins, along with a parodic wink to the double meaning of "Dane" by having an actual Great Dane dog onstage, which also appeared on the production's publicity images.

In OEDIPUS LOVES YOU, THE CRUMB TRAIL and THE REHEARSAL, PLAYING THE DANE, the stage ends up cluttered with all sorts of objects, perhaps symbolising the remains of the troubled minds that they represent. At the same time, this juxtaposition and density of signs forces the audience to choose what piece of information to pay attention to. This "retreat of synthesis"[11] emulates the ways of contemporary life in which the overabundance of information and stimuli—especially through media—renders the perceived world utterly impossible to assimilate as a whole, forcing a "parcelling of perception."[12]

If an impression of disparity prevails in Pan Pan's work, this is intentional, not because it is in line with contemporary approaches to theatre aesthetics, but because it reflects our apprehension of a world addled by superabundant information. Furthermore, these strategies are always embedded in the subject matter at hand, in their tendency to explore the obscure sides of human beings.

OEDIPUS LOVES YOU transposed the Theban family trilogy to contemporary suburbia, portraying a peculiar dysfunctional family in which Tiresias, the blind prophet, is the family counsellor. The set, created by Andrew Clancy, resembled that of MAC-BETH 7, with a large booth made of fibreglass upstage, divided in three sections, representing the kitchen, Jocasta and Oedipus's room and Antigone's. It combined the parody of a family home with the feeling of a mental institution in which the booth compartments resembled both small secure cells and isolation booths in a recording studio. Downstage we found a semi-yard semi-living room with a barbeque, an inflatable pool, armchairs, musical instruments, microphones and other random objects. The chaos of the psyche and its multiplicity were reinforced by two screens above the set, one of them used by Quinn who stood in a sort of DJ cabin next to the sound operator, plotting the scenic action with little figurines while giving instructions to the actors either through messages written and projected on the screen, or through the headphones the actors wore intermittently. This *Deux ex machina* strategy connects clearly to the idea of fate in Greek mythology, while the text establishes links between myth, psychoanalysis and the impossibility of understanding either the human psyche or life's contingency. Ultimately, it is made clear by Pan Pan's reflection that Jocasta's death and Oedipus's blindness relate to a metaphorical state of the soul before the complexities of existence, in a world that is becoming more and more subdued by the values of mediated popular culture.

THE CRUMB TRAIL dealt again with the topic of dysfunctional families, reflecting on the cynicism of detachment brought by media in our lives. It developed and premiered in the Hebbel

Theater in Berlin in the summer of 2008. It was conceived as an installation/performance piece exploring the isolation of floundering for survival in a mediated world in which we try to fulfil our identities. Thus, Hansel and Gretel find themselves lost in a dark forest of media that encompasses projections, live video feed, live YouTube clips and seedy Internet chat rooms. The suggestion of incest through a sex chat room subtly made a comment on child pornography and abuse over the Internet, with a reflection again on those solitary and darker places of the mind. Furthermore, and for anyone living in Ireland, it is hard not to establish a connection to recent State cases against the Catholic Church for child abuse.

The use of lighting through overhead projectors enhanced this idea of dark shadows in human nature. The use of media technology was finely tuned in the dramaturgy being to an extent its central theme. At the same time, the exploration of disconnectedness from reality that virtual worlds create in our lives, played along with the apparently disconnected sequences the script is divided into, and with the scenic action, in which the characters seem unable to communicate to each other in the same space: the family home. Despite its comic and parodic elements, the piece's dominant tone was poignant and violent. As Quinn recognises,

> It was a dark piece. It's about people being alone in their rooms and that particular consciousness reaching out, but actually I think the whole piece is about being lost and asking the philosophical question, can anyone be lost in today's world where you can find anyone in maps, or through GPS? And the other notion: as we are becoming more connected are we becoming less connected? So we are looking at the philosophical heartstrings and the philosophical idea of how we place ourselves and that gave it a very dark atmosphere.

Another usual device of Pan Pan is self-reference, for instance when **THE CRUMB TRAIL** was showed in Project Arts Centre in the very first scene one actor read a review from

The New York Times (where it had been staged in PS 122 before coming to Dublin). In the company's staging of HAMLET, the performance opens with a scholar onstage lecturing on the interpretations of the text, in a similar manoeuvre to MAC-BETH 7. In this sense, Pan Pan also often plays literally with intertextuality, weaving texts from different sources such as *The Dissolution of the Oedipus Complex* by Sigmund Freud in OEDIPUS LOVES YOU, or Beckett's *Endgame* in THE REHEARSAL, PLAYING THE DANE, and the scene between Hamlet and Ophelia in THE CRUMB TRAIL.

Finally, another of Pan Pan's traits is their use of time, which is closely related to their performing style, turning real time into an object of experience. In THE CRUMBTRAIL, OEDIPUS LOVES YOU and THE REHEARSAL, PLAYING THE DANE, the mise-en-scène defies fictional time frames by presenting a continuity of action onstage. Even entrances and exits, which are rare in Pan Pan's work, are not used traditionally to demark a change in action, space or time. For Quinn the use of the fourth dimension relates both to performance style and dramaturgical choices. In terms of acting, the actors are in charge of their own use of time during the performance, according to their own sense of the specific moment. They are not exactly improvising, but reacting to the energy produced by the random encounter between an audience and themselves within the context of the performance event. On the other hand, Quinn also finds that time opens

> dramaturgical doors to different dimensions. [...] it means that you can suddenly switch, you can move, you can flow past into the next idea without having to build all the building blocks along the way.

In their productions this might give a sense of disconnectedness between actions, interruptions that might take place by means of the performers suddenly playing live music onstage (another Pan Pan feature) as in OEDIPUS LOVES YOU and THE CRUMB TRAIL; or a radical change in pace.

But time in Pan Pan has an extra layer. Their performances are in constant flux from inception to the opening throughout touring, playing with the idea of time and liveness by making them co-players of the dramaturgy. Performances not only change from night to night given the nature of the way they work, but from context to context as they tour, in a sort of theatrical plasticity.

Since its inception, Pan Pan has always interrogated the nature of theatre, evolving through fearless experimentation, finding their own stamp within the contemporary milieu of performance aesthetics. One of their greatest achievements is perhaps the ability to be in tune with trends but still have their own trademark and create performance experiences that are very different in form and approach.

This type of work has at times been difficult to digest in Ireland. For Quinn their reception in their home country

> comes and goes. For some performances we've given people feel they don't understand the meaning, because there is an obsession with meaning — as if everything was so straightforward. So in some performances people think that it is too strange or too difficult. Most of the performances we've given have been reasonably popular in one sense. OEDIPUS LOVES YOU was popular although it was probably more popular abroad than it was in Ireland.

Their latest production, the radio play ALL THAT FALL by Samuel Beckett (Project Arts Centre, Dublin, August 2011) is a testimony to that. It had the unmistakable mark of a Pan Pan show by creating a very specific atmosphere achieved by the combination of the superb set and lighting design by Cosgrove, and the precise audio performance and editing by

Quinn. The bare space was covered with a carpet designed for children, on which rocking chairs where placed in scattered patterns, reminiscent of the idea of decay. On each chair the audience found a black cushion with the printing of a skull, an obvious reference to death. From the ceiling hung hundreds of light bulb in a similarly dispersed way. Where we would normally see upstage, light beams formed a square and their illumination responded to the aural experience, moving with the wind, or emulating the shape of an oncoming train. The lead character's steps matched the rhythm of the rocking chairs, and most of the sound effects were made by the same actors—particularly those those of animals.

All these elements blended to create a shared experience with an atmosphere that gave a sense of rift through multiple spaces and times, real and unreal.

1. Gordon Craig, Edward *On the Art of Theatre* (London: Mercury Books, 1962) p.240
2. Féral, Josette "Theatricality: The Specifity of Theatrical Language" in *SubStance* #98/99, 31:2&3 (2002) p.943 www.irishplayography.com/search/play.aspx?la=en&play_id=221
4. Lehmann, Hans-Thies *Postdramatic Theatre*, trans. Karen Jürs-Munby (Oxon: Routledge, 2006).
5. http://theater.nytimes.com/2008/05/24/theater/reviews/24oedi.html
6. Lehmann (2006) p.100
7. ibid. p.104
8. ibid. p.105
9. Lehmann (2006) p.151
10. White, Christine ed., *Directors and Designers* (Bristol & Chicago: Intellect, 2009) p.146
11. Lehmann (2006) p.82
12. ibid. p.88

DISJUNCTION AND THEATRICALITY: ELEVATOR REPAIR SERVICE'S GATZ AND NATURE THEATER OF OKLAHOMA'S NO DICE

FRANCISCO FRAZÃO

ONE

"Often, it began like this." Most reviews of Elevator Repair Service's GATZ include in their initial paragraphs an account of the show's beginning: performer Scott Shepherd arrives in the deserted office that constitutes the set and, after trying and failing to turn on his relic of a computer, finds a copy of F. Scott Fitzgerald's *The Great Gatsby* in a rolodex, which he then proceeds to read out loud. The description usually includes a couple of adjectives for the office (drab, dilapidated, shabby, dingy); it can identify the beverage carried by the office worker (coffee from a Greek Diner, says the New Yorker[1]) and the exact time on the clock that sits atop the computer screen (9:38, according to The New York Times[2]). The sheer number of critical pieces, across continents, has turned this inaugural moment into a recurring motif; and since an entire universe will be evoked through Shepherd's marathon reading of the novel, it is fair to equate the rendering of the show's beginning to a creation myth—a cosmogony.

Describing this unassuming start is clearly convenient: it allows the reviewer to establish that the show takes place in an office (and won't therefore depict the "roaring twenties" glitz usually associated with *Gatsby*), that Shepherd will seamlessly become the narrator Nick Carraway (once he overcomes the initial under-articulation and hesitations), and that the rest of the cast, playing other office workers, will eventually take over the lines of the novel's characters (but, unlike Nick, without recourse to the book). This is the quickest shorthand to explain the rules of the game.

But there's something more to the show's opening move: a childlike fascination ("Boy meets book", writes Ben Brantley[3]). This moment works as an allegory. Elevator Repair Service (ERS) treat Fitzgerald's novel as found material, i.e., a text whose use value was swerved, as it was not intended to become a piece of theatre—and Scott Shepherd's discovery of the book in the rolodex fictionalises the finding of the found text.

One more thing is turned into fiction. Sara Jane Bailes, in a recent book, explores the way failure features as a major generative process in the work of three companies, ERS being one of them. She highlights "the potential gains of an artistic practice characterised by its withdrawal from that which usually signals its success", asserting that "failure is intrinsically linked to the ability to see more and to the expansion of our understanding of an object's properties."[4] It is also a way "to maintain art practice beyond the purview and controlling mechanisms that regulate commercial art production."[5] We can therefore look at the failed attempt to boot up the computer as an allegory of the strategies employed by ERS and others. Not as a strategy exploring the failure of representation, but as a depiction of one: a representation of failure. The broken computer opens up a breach in the everyday, withdrawn from the realm of capitalist productivity, allowing the office space to be permeated by literature. The show's overture, portraying both failure and found text, is a poetics.

"Le plus souvent, ça commençait comme ça." This is the first title card of Jacques Rivette's 1974 film *Céline et Julie vont en bateau*. Julie, sitting on a park bench, reads a treatise on magic and is interrupted by Céline, who scuttles by and drops her sunglasses; Julie follows in pursuit to return them. Rivette is playfully quoting the beginning of *Alice's Adventures in Wonderland*, where the half-hearted reading of a book is replaced by the pursuit of the watch-carrying rabbit. Here fiction becomes possible once reading (Julie's or Alice's) is interrupted, whereas in GATZ the computer replaces the book and the opposite seems to happen. Yet the book might be a portal in all three cases—after all, Julie is learning magic and might have conjured Céline's presence. The difference in GATZ is that Nick takes the book with him for the ride. Commenting on ERS director John Collins's first full-length show, former company member James Hannaham says that, "Every experimental director has to go through an *Alice in Wonderland* thing, and John was very lucky to have gotten his out very early"[6] — yet Scott Shepherd's immersion in the novel's universe may be reminiscent of Alice's plunge down the rabbit-hole.

TWO

Another show, another office; at least judging from the upstage foam-core partitions in the otherwise empty stage, and the mechanical gestures of two performers sitting in their cubicles. "Are you working?/Ohhh yeah!" are the first lines of dialogue, thus placing Nature Theatre of Oklahoma's NO DICE in a diametrically opposed position to GATZ (where the honest answer would be, "Ohhh no!"). In fact, it is hard to summon up two shows that are more dissimilar than these emblematic pieces of New York's recent "downtown theatre" (GATZ opened in Brussels in 2006, NO DICE in NYC in 2007). They seem to embody radically different approaches to text in performance: if GATZ's source material is inescapably literary, NO DICE starts from the everyday, staging an edited array of over 100 hours of phone conversations. (Curiously, the names of the companies invert this dichotomy: Nature Theater of Oklahoma is taken from Kafka's unfinished novel AMERICA, and Elevator Repair Service was the result of a job-aptitude test taken by John Collins when he was a teenager). However, from opposite ends, both pieces dispel or challenge the demands of the dramatic: GATZ through a refusal of adaptation, choosing to include the entire novel, verbatim, thus resisting the pared-down effectiveness of a play;[7] NO DICE with a signal-to-noise ratio much lower than the naturalistic stylisation of dialogue. The two pieces, then,

No Dice — Photo: Peter Nigrini

instead of doing without text altogether (a common misconception of what "postdramatic theatre", to use Hans-Thies Lehmann's famous phrase, is all about), interrogate its status in the context of performance. Text is not something to be transparently and unproblematically put onstage: it is a material that resists and causes friction. And this obstacle is present in the performance, be it the actual book in GATZ or the visible earphones worn by the performers in NO DICE, connected to iPods that continuously feed them their lines.

Besides literature/everyday, another instructive polarity that can be brought to bear on GATZ and NO DICE is one analysed by art critic and historian Michael Fried. The colours used in GATZ's set and lighting[8] bring to mind the paintings of Edward Hopper. There's even a 1940 canvas called "Office at Night" that pictures a man reading at a desk and a woman standing next to a file cabinet, apparently distracted from her immediate task by the man's reading. Fried, talking about a 1755 painting by Jean-Baptiste Greuze called *Un Père de famille qui lit la Bible à ses enfants*, notes how contemporary appraisals admire the concentration of both reader and listeners, as a:

> persuasive representation of a particular state or condition, which each figure in the painting appeared to exemplify in his or her own way, i.e., the state or condition of rapt attention, of being completely occupied or engrossed or (as I prefer to say) absorbed in what he or she is doing, hearing, thinking, feeling.[9]

According to Fried, absorption was a central aspect sought by French painters of the 1750s; in particular, it was imperative that the figures "seem oblivious to the beholder's presence if the illusion of absorption was to be sustained."[10] The opposite stance would have the portrayed figures acknowledging the beholder standing in front of the painting—one judged intolerably theatrical by contemporary sensibilities.

No Dice — Photo: Kelly Cooper

For Fried, the task of the painter in the age of Diderot was to "*de-theatricalise beholding.*"[11] GATZ's office, like Hopper's, appears to belong to this realm of absorption: Nick reading his book and the other workers going about their business; even when the office population is fully-fledged in assuming the roles of the novel's characters, they rarely acknowledge the audience's presence, which would pierce the fourth wall (a Diderot invention, by the way).

In NO DICE, on the other hand, theatricality reigns: the performers often face the audience, exchange worried glances that betray the awareness of being watched, and their acting style is borrowed from 19th century melodrama, or early cinema—before the classical convention of not looking at the camera had been adopted. They also make do with what belongs to a clichéd (and not just Friedian) definition of theatricality: bad foreign accents, vocal excess, wigs and hats. If the set of GATZ can be described as cinematic,[12] the space of NO DICE is inescapably theatrical: the actors hurtle themselves against the walls, they cannot flee theatre's centripetal force; the exits signal a heterogeneous offstage, not a world continuous with what's in sight. Writing about early film, Tom Gunning says its images "rush forward to meet their viewers"[13] (think of the Lumière Brothers' train), thus breaching the screen's surface; and indeed near the end of NO DICE, the performers directly address the spectators and join them in the banked seating.

If early cinema was a fairground attraction, NO DICE is very much interested in peripheral forms of spectacle. Among the topics of conversation are the Moscow Cat Theatre (seen on TV), "dinner theatre" and magic tricks. At one point, performer Anne Gridley re-enacts her favourite movie scene. The moment stands out, firstly because it's in French (sort of) and secondly because it can't conceivably belong to one of the recorded phone conversations that make up the script:

it's a show within the show. In the scene—from Rivette's *Céline et Julie*—Julie takes Céline's place in an audition that can land her a tour to Beirut. In NO DICE, Anne "will imitate Julie...imitating Céline!" Her attempt is no more successful than Julie's: twice removed from the original, like the reflections in Plato's cave, this is a textbook example of the failure of representation.[14]

The homage to *Céline et Julie* has ramifications: there is talk of a magicians' archive, and the "idea for a commercial", with M&Ms that make you dance a specific choreography depending on their colour, is reminiscent of the magic sweets allowing the characters to enter the film's mysterious house (these in turn go back to Alice bottle and cake). Another Rivettian nod is in Nature Theatre's publicity materials for the show, which announce "a short four-hour version of their legendary 11-hour melodramatic spectacle"[15] (Rivette's OUT 1 has a 13-hour long version and a "short" one, SPECTRE, that lasts five hours.)[16] But perhaps the greatest similarity between Rivette's work and that of Nature Theater (and indeed ERS's) is one of process. For his 1969 film *L'Amour Fou*, he delegated the staging of a play and the shooting of a documentary about it and filmed the result. Nature Theater, instead of painstakingly blocking the entire piece, established rules. Says co-director Kelly Copper:

> In NO DICE the actors had to: 1) Keep the exact language and timing of the recorded phone calls; 2) Keep the accent going; 3) Use eyes and melodramatic emotion to extract the biggest drama from the material; 4) Use one of the three sets of hand gestures we created; and 5) Be in one of thirteen paired positions on stage.[17]

ERS similarly challenge themselves with each new project: read an entire novel onstage (GATZ); make a show almost entirely in the dark (ROOM TONE); systematically paraphrase the dialogue of a play (CAB LEGS). All these rules, big and small, contribute to make the production more about process than artefact; they release it from some of the pitfalls of intention and the creative genius; and they further subvert representation's chain of command.

Returning to absorption/theatricality: the contrast between GATZ and NO DICE is, of course, not as clearcut as Fried's dichotomy. In fact, I would argue, both shows, each in their fashion, contribute to a deconstruction, or supersession, of this polarity. Among GATZ's moments of blatant theatricality it's easy to pick the entire paragraph in Chapter 3 mimicked by Susie Sokol: "[...] A celebrated tenor had sung in Italian, and a notorious contralto had sung in jazz, and between the numbers people were doing 'stunts' all over the garden [...]"[18] Sokol's slapstick illustration is just such a succession of stunts and numbers: like Anne imitating Julie imitating Céline, it's a spectacle within a spectacle, and about spectacle. And when near the end of the show Shepherd abandons the book and recites the whole final chapter, for the first time not reading, it's difficult to say if theatricality finally supplanted absorption or if absorption, taken to its last consequences, has simply morphed into delicate, exhilarating, melancholy theatre.

As for NO DICE, can't the earphoned performers be seen as a figure of absorption just as much as Scott Shepherd bent over his book, listening instead of reading, an emblem of the iPod age where you go "through your day…hearing music constantly?"[19] Co-director Pavol Liska says the following:

> I'm interested in attention as opposed to concentration. If somebody is just concentrated it shuts them down. I as a human being want to increase the number of things that I pay attention to around me, and that's what I want my actors to do. I want them to propose to the audience a way of living.[...] So what I look for in performers is their ability to be sensitised to as many things as possible.[...] I try to increase the number of tasks that they have to deal with at every single moment so they can't concentrate; they can only pay attention.[20]

DISJUNCTION AND THEATRICALITY

Halfway between absorption and theatricality, then: or a centrifugal attention that produces theatre. The accurate emblem for this centaur should thus be the severed earphones used in the show, only inserted in one ear, so that the actor is at once there and elsewhere, present but "borne back ceaselessly into the past".

THREE

It might be worth considering what impact Michael Fried's famous 1967 essay "Art and Objecthood", an indictment of minimalist art (which he calls "literalist"), has for this discussion. In it, minimalist work is seen as a threat to modernism, and disparagingly described as "theatre". It's difficult to equate the industrial solids of Robert Morris, Tony Smith or Donald Judd with 18th century figurative painting—their theatre must be much more abstract and essential. Indeed, its definition can persuasively describe not only visual arts minimalism but also the contemporary practice of Cunningham and Cage, the Judson Dance Theater and a whole avant-garde cluster whose influence extends to the work of both ERS and Nature Theater. For Fried "the experience of literalist art is of an object in a situation—one that, virtually by definition, includes the beholder"[21]; there's a "special complicity that the work extorts from the beholder. Something is said to have presence when it demands that the beholder take it into account"[22]; furthermore, the beholder's experience of the work "persists in time, and the presentment of endlessness that, I have been claiming, is central to literalist art and theory is essentially a presentment of endless or indefinite duration. [...]"[23] Experience, situation, complicity, presence, duration are keywords that can be applied with equal success to Tony Smith's *Cube Die* and other things that are, well, not dice, like John Cage's 4'33" or a performance by Marina Abramovic. In an interview, John Collins reflects on ERS's use of literature:

> the best way for us to bring literature to our theatrical language is to bring it in wholly and make it an experience, as opposed to repeating it as literature, as a lesser literary achievement, or a condensation or an imitation or an impression of a work of literature. Make it something that is entirely an experience and something that is also complete and whole in its literariness.[24]

Elsewhere he speaks of keeping the book's "bookness". I've already mentioned the way both companies treat language in the theatre as friction, and Fried mentions the literalist object's "obtrusiveness". Text is therefore taken in its entirety, a block of language as solid as Smith's cube. There is a refusal of adaptation but, I would argue, also of translation,[25] at least of the idea of translation that implies loss and signal degradation (perhaps a better analogy would be that of quotation). In NO DICE, the language itself is abstracted: there is an attempt to record the "cosmic murmur" that goes unnoticed, the meanings behind a "uh-huh" can be endlessly debated and all the "Ums", "Mmms", "Uhs" and "likes" attain an eerie materiality.

Of course, duration plays a big role in this process. Both shows far exceed the "two hours' traffic of our stage", or our attention span's one hour (NO DICE is four hours long, GATZ six), and it's that length that turns them into an experience, something you live through and not just watch. So even though both pieces treat their texts as found material, they are far from being readymade: they take time. However, it's probably misleading to describe these as durational events, such as those, for instance, of Forced Entertainment's output. They seem to allegorise duration itself, to talk about it. In NO DICE, the non-existent 11-hour version of the show hovers like a spectre over the actual performance; they threaten to skip the interval if sponsorship isn't found; and the editing of the material itself, while putting together many different dialogues, produces in the audience the lived experience of having been privy to one long conversation. As for GATZ, there's that stopped clock that continually taunts us,[26] and a gap between the time of reading and the time of the narrative: the show can embody the former but only represent the latter, as in Wilson's long night after his wife's murder. So these pieces simultaneously subvert a bourgeois audience's expectations of a night at the theatre and a hardcore one's habituation to the stringencies of the durational. Time is here both an experience and a representation.

Disjunction is perhaps the most important shared device between GATZ and NO DICE. The 1986 New York Times review of Heiner Müller's HAMLETMACHINE (directed by Robert Wilson) says: "We hear Müller's voice; we see Wilson's vision. Both run on simultaneous tracks."[27] Postdramatic theatre exposes the seamlessness between text and production for the ideological construct that it is, replacing coherence and cohesion with an aesthetics of mismatch.

Reviewing GATZ, Peter Crawley uses a writing analogy (palimpsest) and one from photography (double exposure) to describe the juxtaposition of the world of the office and that of the novel.[28] The presence of both realms allows for all sorts of modalities: coincidence, commentary, illustration, interference, interruption or mere co-existence; one world can recede into oblivion and reappear later with the starkness of a (literal) neon light (sound and light design are paramount in this negotiation). The release from the dictates of coherence also makes room for ERS's signature (and joyous) eclecticism: the soundtrack includes "Duke Ellington, Kronos Quartet, and the Afro-Cuban All Stars"[29]; a sofa can be a piano, an inflatable mattress, a coffin and a sofa; the production's style can go from frantic slapstick (when Nick has Gatsby and Daisy for tea), to child play (when the Finn brings said tea), to film-noir pastiche (when there's a hint that Gatsby killed a man), to subdued drama (as in the shaded hotel room in chapter 7), to utter dejection and emptiness (the long night of chapter 8).

Yet we always return to the basic investigation (epistemological in nature): what happens to theatre when it really lets literature in? The outcome is surprisingly freeing. A conventional adaptation would be at a complete loss if it had to "translate" a passage like this one, about Gatsby's smile:

> It was one of those rare smiles with a quality of eternal reassurance in it, that you may come across four or five times in life. It faced — or seemed to face — the whole eternal world for an instant, and then concentrated on you with an irresistible prejudice in your favour. It understood you just so far as you wanted to be understood, believed in you as you would like to believe in yourself, and assured you that it had precisely the impression of you that, at your best, you hoped to convey.[30]

In GATZ, it's enough for Scott Shepherd to read it and Jim Fletcher to smile. Another interesting challenge has to do with the gap between the two times in play. For instance here:

> Gatsby, his hands still in his pockets, was reclining against the mantelpiece in a strained counterfeit of perfect ease, even of boredom. His head leaned back so far that it rested against the face of a defunct mantelpiece clock, and from this position his distraught eyes stared down at Daisy[...].
>
> 'We've met before,' muttered Gatsby. His eyes glanced momentarily at me, and his lips parted with an abortive attempt at a laugh.[31]

What in narrative time shouldn't last more than a few moments takes considerably longer to read; by having Jim Fletcher strictly follow the choreography, and holding the position for as long as it takes to describe it, there's an opportunity for a gag, but also for the perfect embodiment of Gatsby's awkwardness. Failure to match both rhythms results in the passage's exact materialisation (and in the process even the broken clock that had been sitting on top of the computer since the beginning of the show is accounted for).

DISJUNCTION AND THEATRICALITY

From an initial position of mismatch, illumination can arise. The same goes for the office setting. Rebecca Mead sees it as "an objective correlative for Nick Carraway's, and Fitzgerald's, disillusionment"[32], but this interpretation is a tentative endpoint and not a given. It's not an illustration nor a metaphor for *The Great Gatsby*; it is, to begin with, *something else*, anything else. That's the only way it can become its truth. The same can be said for the show's title (James GATZ is the real name of Jay Gatsby) and for Fletcher's performance: "In his charmless, joyless demeanour, one senses the strain, the effort and the monotony behind the façade of his existence as Gatsby."[33] Coherence at last (perhaps we can't help it), but emerging out of intriguing discrepancy.

The title of NO DICE has at least two explanations, one idiomatic and one literal: it is a reply to Sarah Benson's commission, who wanted Nature Theater to stage *Twelfth Night* at Soho Rep and got this show instead; it is a comment on the chance mechanism used to make decisions about the choreography—if for the previous show (POETICS: A BALLET BRUT) dice had been used, this time it was cards…There are:

> three suits of gestures: one from a magician DVD, one of disco dance moves, and one based on a sign language invented by Pavol's mother during the times when, sitting on rehearsal, she wanted to tell the actors (who spoke less Slovak than she did English) a story. The fourth and final suit is populated by thirteen of the most common two-person theater and soap opera positions[…].[34]

What look like random sets of observed movement contribute in subtle ways to the piece's cohesion: the magician's gestures connect to *Céline et Julie*; the disco to the M&Ms advertisement; and Pavol's mother's sign language responds to the show's preoccupation with storytelling—"You know any good stories?" is a recurring question that never gets a satisfying answer. Yet not knowing during the performance

Gatz — Photo: Gene Pittman/Mark Barton

where the hand gestures come from renders them at once funny, hypnotic and disquieting. They stress specific words, as in everyday conversation, but the connection between iconic content and verbal material seems to belong to an ever-changing secret code, a Kafkaesque nightmare.

Recourse to chance and disjunction comes straight from the practice of Cage and Cunningham, where the musical score and choreography were sometimes produced separately and only met on opening night. Here this isn't exactly a formal experiment, a decantation of the artform's components, but a game and a struggle for actors and audience alike. The performance operates on several simultaneous tracks: the verbal content, the hammy acting style of Robert Johanson, Zachary Oberzan and Anne Gridley, the accents (Jamaican, Irish and French) that come and go, the costumes (a pirate with Hasidic sidelocks, a moustachioed cowboy, a red-haired showgirl) and the choreography. The result is a complex score of dissonance, with moments of sudden harmony: there's a burst of recognition (melodramatic and metatheatrical) when a policeman with a bad Irish accent and another who's a Hasidic Jew are mentioned as part of a dinner theatre show…

FOUR

Rivette once said that a fiction film is always a documentary of its own shooting. We've already looked at some of the self-reflexive moments in GATZ and NO DICE: the representation of duration in a durational piece, the concern with other forms of spectacle. NO DICE is actually structured like one of those forms (dinner theatre): the directors offer the audience sandwiches before the start, as well as beverages (Diet Coke and Dr. Pepper, which will feature right in the first scene); and during the break, as in dinner theatre, we can buy dessert (yes, M&Ms).

FRANCISCO FRAZÃO

The chief metatheatrical statements, however, concern process, as with GATZ's initial allegory of failure and the finding of found text. Here is where, according to John Collins, the office comes from: "I held a few rehearsals with two actors [...] in a cramped little office above a small downtown theatre. We decided to use that crummy office as an imaginative setting for the reading of the book."[35] And the costumes in NO DICE, according to Kelly Copper: "We needed something that could transform that material, so we asked them [the actors] to find costumes in the back of the theatre. (We were working at Downtown Art, a local youth theatre, and they had a lot of great costumes)."[36] Both shows know where they come from, and honour that memory (yet another explanation for the title GATZ). But these are also private jokes (they help shape a community among the creative team), although imbued with generosity (a mystery, something precious, is presented to us). The link between private signified and public signifier was severed, although an undercurrent of meaning transforms the random into mysterious.

Another exploration of process relates to the presence onstage of both source texts (one written, the other aural, both accessible to us only indirectly): like an objectified prompter, it guarantees that they are rendered verbatim. This replicates the process of rehearsal, when actors don't know their lines (although Scott Shepherd has memorised the entire novel). When, for the last chapter, Shepherd goes off-book, there is finally no gap between him and his character; and the show ends.

In "The Emancipated Spectator", Jacques Rancière says, "it is high time we examine this idea that the theatre is, in and of itself, a community site. [...] This presupposition continues to precede theatrical performances and anticipate its effects."[37] These shows do the opposite: everything they achieve is the result of a journey, not an *a priori* effect. Exploring essential components of the theatrical experience (presence, disjunction, duration, metamorphosis), they don't take them for granted—it's the fetishisation of co-presence between actors and spectators what causes the self-indulgent idea of community Rancière rebukes. Near the end of NO DICE, the actors remove their wigs and hats and address the audience: it seems a moment of absolute, untampered sincerity—and in a way it is—but their lines ("Words of Encouragement" in the transcript) are still being fed through the earphones, and have been heard twice before, so it's really a re-presentation. The beauty is that, because of the low-tech nature of the show, the iPods have gone out of sync, and what we hear is not an ideal community speaking in unison but one made of quietly discordant solitary voices. They beat on, in GATZ and in NO DICE, "against the current".

1. Mead, Rebecca *Adaptation*, New Yorker (27 September 2010)
2. Brantley, Ben *Borne back ceaselessly into the past*, The New York Times (6 October 2010)—http://theater.nytimes.com/2010/10/07/theater/reviews/07gatz.html?pagewanted=all
3. Ibid.
4. Bailes, Sara Jane *Performance Theatre and the Poetics of Failure—Forced Entertainment*, Goat Island, Elevator Repair Service (London and New York: Routledge, 2011) p.11
5. Ibid., p.106
6. Mead, Rebecca op. cit.
7. Trueman, Matt criticises ERS's later show *The Select* for rubbing against "the streamlined nature of drama" ("Review: The Sun Also Rises (The Select), Lyceum Theatre", *Carousel of Fantasies*, 16 August 2010—http://carouseloffantasies.blogspot.com/2010/08/review-sun-also-rises-select-lyceum.html). But discussing Gatz he states approvingly that "What quickly becomes apparent is how ill-fitted it [the novel] is for the stage." ("Review: Gatz, Public Theatre, New York", ibid., 26 November 2010—http://carouseloffantasies.blogspot.com/2010/11/gatz-public-theatre-new-york.html)
8. By Louisa Thompson and Mark Barton, respectively. Rebecca Mead, op. cit.
9. Fried, Michael *Absorption and Theatricality—Painting and Beholder in the Age of Diderot* (Chicago and London: The University of Chicago Press) p.10
10. Ibid., p.66
11. Ibid., p.104
12. Its widescreen shape, the frames within the frame of door, windowed cubicle and corridor in the back, the way the shelves stage left disappear into the wings and suggest an unseen but homogeneous fictional universe...
13. Gunning, Tom "An aesthetic of astonishment: early film and the (in)credulous spectator", *Art & Text* (Spring 1989) p.36

14 The "poetics of failure" might just be what separates contemporary experimental theatre from postdramatic staples like Robert Wilson. Chris Goode: "Wilson's hard line [...] admits no room for error or for chance. Which to my mind is tantamount to saying, it refuses love." ("'Bob': a job; plus, To 'Hell'and back", *Thompson's Bank of Communicable Desire*, 24 February, 2007 — http://beescope.blogspot.com/2007/02/bob-job-plus-to-hell-and-back.html)
15 Nature Theater of Oklahoma, *No Dice* (programme notes) (Brussels: Kaaitheater, 2008)
16 Out 1's structure, divided in episodes like the early cinematic serials, is as an inspiration to Nature Theater's current project, *Life and Times*.
17 Young-Jean Lee, "Nature Theater of Oklahoma", *BOMB* (Summer 2009) http://bombsite.com/issues/108/articles/3303
18 Fitzgerald, F. Scott *The Great Gatsby* (London:Penguin, 1992) p.47
19 Nature Theater of Oklahoma, *No Dice* (New York: 53rd State Press, 2007) p.29
20 Benson, Sarah "Working Downtown", *PAJ: A Journal of Performance and Art* (PAJ 83, Volume 28, Number 2, May 2006) pp. 51–52
21 Fried, Michael "Art and Objecthood", *Art and Objecthood — Essays and Reviews* (Chicago and London: The University of Chicago Press) p.153
22 Ibid., p.155
23 Ibid., pp.166–167
24 Philip Bither, *Elevator Repair Service's Gatz* (Minneapolis: Walker Art Center, 2008) — http://www.elevator.org/press/story.php?show=gatz&story=walker_interview

25 Even though Sara Jane Bailes, in her review of the piece, says "We translate (rather than adapt) the novel" ("Gatz", *Theatre Journal*, Volume 59, Number 3, October 2007, p. 508), the distinction here doesn't seem to be helpful.
26 Kelly Copper reminded me the set of No Dice also has a clock — one that keeps good time.
27 Gussow, Mel "Stage View; Cranking Up a Powerful Hamletmachine", The New York Times (25 May 1986) — http://theater.nytimes.com/mem/theater/treview.html. There's a slight lack of precision here (we don't actually hear Müller's voice, as sound is as much a part of the show as all of Wilson's imagery), but the idea is clear.
28 Crawley, Peter "Review of Gatz at the Project", Irish Times (29 September 2008) — http://www.elevator.org/press/story.php?show=gatz&story=irishtimes1
29 Bailes, Sara Jane *Gatz*, p.508.
30 Fitzgerald, F. Scott op. cit., pp.48–49
31 Ibid., p.84
32 Mead, Rebecca op. cit.
33 Trueman, Matt "Review: Gatz, Public Theatre, New York"
34 Reed, Amber "Introduction", *No Dice*, p.8
35 Collins, John "Director's Note: A history of ERS and The Great Gatsby, and Gatz" (Brussels: Kunstenfestivaldesarts, 2006) — http://archive.kfda.be/2006/en/projectdetail.action-projectid=12650&id=340.htm
36 Young-Jean Lee, op. cit.
37 Jacques Rancière, *The Emancipated Spectator* (London and New York: Verso, 2009) p.16

This is how you will disappear
Photo: Seldon Hunt

ESSAY 8

GISÈLE VIENNE: THE STAGE OF DESIRE

CHANTAL HURAULT (TRANS. MICHAEL WEST)

THE FASCINATION WITH DISTURBANCE

Populated with lifeless mannequins, production after production of Gisèle Vienne's work plays on the disturbance of presences hovering between life and death. A troubling blend of the familiar and the strange—the very embodiment of Freud's concept of the Uncanny—her work follows in a direct line from Kantor's Theatre of Death which opened up modern theatre to the laws of incompatibilites. The incompleteness of the marionette being intrinsic to its plastic and dramatic charge, Gisèle Vienne is less interested in the magic of manipulation than in the disturbance it releases.

> Anthropomorphic forms lose none of the disturbance they generate; they are to be found everywhere in the contemporary scene together with the need for human reproduction through this media, the puppet.[1]

The stage, as a place of simulacra, in I APOLOGIZE (2004), reconstructs an accident in which a space-time permeated by a desire for death, dolls and mannequins exist in a bewitching hybridity.

Already featured in JERK (2008), the ventriloquist's dummy is at the centre of her latest creation, the first in a series entitled LAST SPRING—created in collaboration with the American writer Dennis Cooper, with whom she has been working since 2004—whose architecture and dramaturgy draw inspiration from haunted houses and virtual spaces. LAST SPRING: A PREQUEL (2011) features a lifesize ventriloquist's dummy of a teenager who enacts a schizophrenic dialogue with a glove puppet it holds in its hand. The borders here are particularly porous: when the mannequin's body is still, its appearance is terrifyingly human. When the puppet "speaks", the mannequin's hand waves it mechanically and violently. Held by the feet, head down, it reminds us constantly of its inanimate state. These two "actors" point up the monstros-

GISÈLE VIENNE: THE STAGE OF DESIRE

ity of the other, as if both were vying to be the primary, all-knowing—and therefore living—voice. "Charles is dead. This performance is his relic," says the puppet, speaking of a "mutant", of an "accident of nature", all the while presenting itself as "a magician". In response, the mannequin wonders: "Am I a projection of myself", "a double"? And then, as if to emphasise the demiurge-like, diabolical quality of the puppet in its hand, the mannequin asks "[Is it] a machine? Unless it's possessed…"

The second installation of **LAST SPRING** will continue exploring this disturbing relationship with the body. In a maze, the solitary audience member will come across artificial teenagers, embodied and disembodied, in a series of enactments or "a spectrum of animation-states" which sometimes "enliven them, or kill them, or return them to the status of objects," says Gisèle Vienne. For some time now her photographic work, like her work with dolls and mannequins, has interrogated the intensities of life through body-objects. Is it possible to kill a doll?

The unsettling strangeness, the process of moving from a mechanical body to a liberated body, inscribes a new artistic form. **SHOWROOMDUMMIES**, one of her first pieces (created with Étienne Bideau-Rey in 2001 and remounted in a new version in 2009), blends the real with the unreal in a poetics of the body. In the performance, a masked woman (a revealing character of this type of hybridity) embodies a non-unified, disintegrated nature. If the mask freezes the possibility of movement, even in stillness the fixed expression of the smile reanimates it.

As in **A PREQUEL**, the most shocking aspect of these complex identities is their essentially disturbing duality, simultaneously animate and inanimate. Imposing an image onto a body that slips away from us, Gisèle Vienne creates fantasy characters in which we are unable to untangle the real from the imagined. Ceaselessly switching back and forth between the impression of life given off by the mannequins and the sense of death which envelops the actors, everything hinges on the fact of simultaneity.

IMPOSSIBLE BODIES

Among the many authors who inspire Gisèle Vienne, Sacher-Masoch holds a vital place. **SHOWROOMDUMMIES** explicitly references *Venus in Furs*. The ceremonial of punishment, the delight in pain and humiliation, the type known in psychoanalysis as the masochist all appear in **I APOLOGIZE** and **UNE BELLE ENFANT BLONDE** (2005). **SHOWROOMDUMMIES** tackles the fascination with the dominatrix with a disturbing inertia. On stage there is no Venus as such, but shop window mannequins, a "mass produced" Wanda. If we see something of a statue of Venus in the icy nature of Wanda and her perfect beauty, the stylised body, a deconsecrated icon, blandly alludes to a contemporary 'ideal' of the sex trade. In its distancing from the everyday it explicitly invokes the fantasy world of Pierre Molinier. Finding artistic expression in excessive sexual perversions, in its fetishist erotism, its immoral surrealism, **SHOWROOMDUMMIES** furthers Molinier's desire to "define" through his photomontages the image of the ideal woman, the woman who will give him ultimate satisfaction who he will tirelessly reconstruct "from scattered pieces taken from a series of separate bodies."[2] The piece interrogates the influence of the representation of the body on our erotic imagination, which takes stereotypes and from them fashions new idealised figures.

Petrified bodies and animated dolls create a theatre of disorder which leads from the living body to the image, knowing that immobility is for Gisèle Vienne an "ultimate tipping over into the unreal."* In a relentless rupture, fluid dance and realistic games are violently fragmented, disembodied. This choreographic language joins living and inanimate figures in the same fragile and violent state where the body *becomes* the image. The combination of the instincts for life and death acts together on everything.

In the realms of art and erotism, dolls and mannequins are fetish objects, charged with a heavy history of contradictions, which, in their transgressive or immoral aspects, touch on religion as well as the marketplace. Again and again, dolls in skirts and blazers, legs spread open to the public, carelessly display their innnocence. A timeless image of the young girl, with its expressionless face the doll appears in its erotic and provocative form. Obsessional, both forbidden and available, she is close to the emotional disorder of LES JEUX DE LA POUPÉE (THE GAMES OF THE DOLL) by Hans Bellmer, an impossible, even morbid, body. We are at the heart of the contradiction between the forbidden and the transgression on which Georges Bataille bases his concept of erotism and Gisèle Vienne her work.

The age old motif of the dead girl is one of the most lively interfaces between erotism and death. ÉTERNELLE IDOLE (2009) continues the fascination with the close yet remote body, strangely present, horribly absent. Staging this play in a skating rink is a strong and symbolic choice. On a set of ice, the skater — the ghost of a murdered Lolita — connects the eternal with the present moment. From her phantom state to that of the image she imposes her innocence in a fantasy form.

While the recurring character of Lolita appears from Nabokov to Robbe-Grillet, the eternal idol of Gisèle Vienne is more directly influenced by Laura Palmer of David Lynch's *Twin Peaks*. The dead body shows itself in a supreme beauty. Its innocence reveals a troubling erotism. Gisèle Vienne adds to the image of Lolita her male double—a young and handsome man, a slightly lost, rather desperate slacker. A familiar figure from the 90s and the work of Gus Van Sant and, of course, the George Miles character in the work of Dennis Cooper. These twin figures, locked in combat, meet again in THIS IS HOW YOU WILL DISAPPEAR (2010). Whether from innocence or suicidal despair, a tension of opposing forces is set up, innocence vs corruption, beauty vs. decay. Beauty brings with it the desire to profane it, the essence of erotism is linked to defilement, and the final meaning of erotism: death.

THE EXPERIENCE OF TRANSGRESSION

The links between erotic desire and death oppose other irreconcilables—the forbidden and the transgression, Bataille's "blind point," where erotism reaches its extremity. Crime is the principal form of transgression, Sade finding in it the most voluptuous satisfaction. To attain absolute, unwavering desire, the greatest libertines refuse to submit to lesser climaxes. In *Lautréamont et Sade*, Maurice Blanchot speaks of a cruelty which "is pure self-negation, taken so far that it transforms into a destructive explosion, a numbness that makes the entire being shudder." In the violence of this negation, the cold-blooded crime stirs up an absolute effervescence of pleasure. It situates the being in a movement of transgression which won't stop until it reaches the summit of transgression.

The relationship of the imagination to the fantasy and the impossibility of its realisation is the starting point for UNE BELLE ENFANT BLONDE. At the heart of the piece is the testimony of the writer Catherine Robbe-Grillet. On stage, a mature, composed woman shares her fantasies, talks of the fetishism of the knife, recollects her adventures to appease her fantasies—much as Robbe-Grillet does in the novel *Women's Rites*, under her pseudonym Jeanne de Berg[3]—while the body of a black man is hacked open with a knife. We pass from narration to enactment. Reminiscence and fiction mingle in a "mise-en-abîme" of the individualisation of fantasy. The fact that the text is written by Dennis Cooper further decentres the autobiographic "I" and robs Catherine Robbe-Grillet of her experience. Moreover, by abandoning her personal account in favour of the enactment—that is to say, by leaving the realm of the past for the concrete and present one of the performance—the fantasy acquires a timeless quality. This displacement climaxes at the end of the spectacle when, after the murder scene, the blonde child returns onstage alone and plays a recording which repeats the murder—a sonar image which perpetuates the violence.

In A PREQUEL, a performance with an animatronic mannequin and a glove puppet, we hear the first and last words of the boy, haunted by the murdering puppet: "Wait! Listen to me. I need your help." "Please, save me! Please!" The effect of the loop emphasises the artifice of the representation. The boy even adds, "Why doesn't that ring true?" We gradually forget the blond boy is a blue-eyed mannequin—whose eyelashes open and close…Taunted by the mischevious voice which speaks of the "mutilated body" it finally appears in before us as a wandering soul, devastated by violent, timeless memories.

Far from being an apologia for erotic crimes, and without moralizing, the criminal or sexual disorder is treated from a sensitive point of view, associated with theatricalisation of fantasy. When Bataille recounts, in detail, the murders of children by Gilles de Rais in *The Tears of Eros*, describing the spilled entrails of the most beautiful bodies, he makes clear that the mere act of evoking it makes him retch. But he draws from this the importance of facing what mankind really is. If Christianity has shied away from this type of representation, and if the marketplace abuses it in a modern

Showroomdummies — Photo: Mathilde Darel

form of slavery, the challenge is to present to the onlooker what cannot be looked at.

As with Sade, whom Bataille describes as the first "interior observer", this allows us to think the unthinkable, to understand what underpins it at the same time as that which undermines it. Attached to the world surrounding her, the work of Gisèle Vienne marks out in this sense the "storm of desire" to open our consciousness to self-awareness.

THE SPACE OF DESIRE

Revisiting the Apollonian and Dionysian beauty of Nietzsche, **THIS IS HOW YOU WILL DISAPPEAR** explores the beauty deriving from order and disorder. **I APOLOGIZE** already responded to the unease in our society, torn between a desire for sterilisation and the excesses of drugs and prostitution. The connection between order and chaos, beauty and ruin—recalling the Romantic tradition—places three characters in a crisis which reveals to each of them their solitude. It is not a matter of dubbing the world but to absorb its violence and excess. As in **KINDERTOTENLIEDER** (2007), we are in a hyper-real forest; the exterior landscape reinforces the scenic frame. The spiritual quest of characters is linked to a desire for unity with the world, but, if at first it protects itself behind the illusion of a benevolent nature, by the end it exacerbates this idyllic dream in savage nature. The production starts with a young female athlete training under the watchful eye of her "master", both of them in tyrannical pursuit of perfection.

An initial aesthetic contradiction crosses these identities: the experience of beauty relies on imperfection. The arrival of a third character, the young rock star, provokes an internal conflict which tips the play into darkness. All are imbued with immoderate desire to test their limits, only one thinks of death as a solution to despair. The boy is a double of

Goethe's Werther, the brother of Kurt Cobain. Fascinated by the obscure beauty of the boy but overwhelmed by a feeling of repulsion, the trainer is faced with another relationship to death, one that is no longer arousing, but suicidal. Driven by a morbid erotism he discloses his most intimate thoughts, weeps, and beats him to death. The action does not reside in the violence of the depiction but in the inner impulse of the man, himself a victim. It is not a natural violence but one described by Bataille as that of "a being of reason who tries to obey, but succumbs to the impulse which in himself he cannot reduce to reason." The harmony between man and nature melts away in the instant of this encounter. In the grip of chaos he is aware of his inner turmoil.

The athlete who seeks by the pain of her physical exploits to attain her ideal of beauty, wavers in turn, swept away into a mystic crisis. In a state of shock, prostrate, a distant song "as if coming out of the depths"* escapes from her body. Motionless, against a tree, she stares at the ground where the boy lies, bloody but still alive. In a reference to the final scene of **UNE BELLE ENFANT BLONDE** where the recording prolongs the murder scene, this spontaneous, quasi-religious song is a continuation of the murder of the young man. The athlete is unrealised in the vision of the mutilated body. If our desires and our repulsions are provoked by an aesthetic experience emerging from the tension of opposites, the discovery of a corpse is the source of a shattering poetic experience. This type of excess, mystical or artistic, leads to the "inner experience" in Bataille's terminology, that is, the sensation of *indistinction* of the body in the world.

The poetic path reveals the infinite territory of desire. Since **SHOWROOMDUMMIES**, Gisèle Vienne has tackled the confusion produced by the Venus of Sacher-Masoch. Through the multiplication of statues, paintings and "real" encounters she has found a primordial identification between the erotic and the artistic disturbance. "From the body to the work of art, from the work of art to Ideas, there is an ascension which should be made to the lash of the whip,"[4] writes Deleuze. THIS IS HOW YOU WILL DISAPPEAR revisits these "supra-sensual" beings submitted to the law of opposites. With young Werther, rediscovered in George Miles, the fantasy is "at the crossroads of fundamental violences", Bataille's priviledged site.

THIS IS HOW YOU WILL DISAPPEAR is a quest for spiritual truth through sensory and physical experience. LAST SPRING pursues this labyrinthine quest with the intention to move the spectator's gaze from the physical reality to a "space of mental perceptions." When Gisèle Vienne turned from philosophy to the theatre, she chose to develop her thinking through concrete work on the stage: "To take the body and physical experience into consideration allows us to have complete sight over what drives us, including that which we repress and which feeds our thoughts."* She has constructed a theatrical language capable of inducing contradictory sensations without ever reducing the image to a closed horizon. The sense escapes, the text remains sometimes inaudible. Neither interpretation nor justification, as if the theatre stage becomes an elusive space, containing that which is irreducible in desire — which resists all direct solicitation. Fantasy participates and destroys the real, its theatricalisation puts into perspective a supremacy of the body. The stage appears as a foreclosed space where we comes face to face with irrational impulses. To open up the space peculiar to desire is also perhaps to invent a philosophy of the body.

GISÈLE VIENNE: THE STAGE OF DESIRE

1. Vienne, Gisèle interview with Chantal Hurault, 29 January 2010. Quotations marked by an asterisk (*) come from the same interview.
2. For Pierre Molinier see the work of Pierre Petit, Molinier, une vie d'enfer, Ramsey/Jean-Jacques Pauvert, 1992.
3. de Berg, Jeanne *Women's Rites* (London: Grove Press, 1987)
4. Originally *Présentation de Sacher-Masoch*, 1967 (in *Masochism*—includes "Coldness and Cruelty" by Gilles Deleuze and "Venus in Furs," the original novel by Leopold von Sacher-Masoch (Elzunidor, 2005).

Neutral Hero — Photo: Almudena Crespo

ESSAY 9

WITHOUT GUILE: RICHARD MAXWELL AND THE NEW YORK CITY PLAYERS

Drummer Wanted – Photo: Michael Schmelling

SARAH GORMAN

The work of Richard Maxwell tends to polarise critics and audience members alike. Some find his actors' uninflected mode of delivery and static demeanour unsatisfactory and alienating, while others find his tendency towards minimalism lends insight into the tenderness of barely perceptible gestures and beauty in the mundane exchanges of everyday life. Notwithstanding this ambiguity of critical reception, his work has been acclaimed internationally, recognised as offering a compelling and challenging contribution to contemporary experimental theatre.

Maxwell and his company, The New York City Players (NYCP), are based in New York. Over the past twenty-two years he has written and directed over twenty plays and has recently set up the American Playwrights Division, an initiative to produce the work of new playwrights in association with NYCP. Originally working with Cook County Theater Department in Chicago, he moved to New York in the mid-nineties to forge his own pathway into the experimental theatre scene. His work has received plaudits both at home and abroad; NYCP was invited to perform as part of the Venice Biennale (2005) and he receives regular commissions from major European venues. He won an Obie for **HOUSE** in 1999, with other company members gaining Obie recognition for their contribution to **GOOD SAMARITANS** (2005) and **HOUSE**. Maxwell has recently been selected for a Guggenheim Fellowship and has received awards from the Foundation for Contemporary Arts and the Best in Festival Award at Zürcher Theater Spektakel.

Maxwell initially gained recognition in Europe with productions such as **HOUSE** (1998), **BOXING 2000** (2000), **JOE** (2002) and **DRUMMER WANTED** (2002), pieces which feature gauche and uncertain young men who converse in idiosyncratic quasi-adolescent vernacular. The aspirations they express suggest that these characters want to "go places", but they lack the wherewithal to transform their surroundings and are often robbed of the gift of articulation when trying to communicate their desires to others. For Markus Wessendorf, Maxwell's characters remind him of "losers in a society that reveres self-exposure."[1] Songs, usually soft-rock ballads, represent a key component of these plays. Well-crafted melodies give the characters an opportunity to voice and make sense of the inner turmoil they are experiencing. These pieces, as with others, saw Maxwell casting an amalgamation of experienced and inexperienced actors, incorporating the "real" signs of their labour as they worked to make sense of a monologue or strained to hit the high notes. Maxwell would invite the experienced actors to temporarily forget their training and to consider what it might mean to come to the project of acting afresh, having been denuded of the skills and coping strategies taught in college.[2] For him, the "industry standard" Method Acting taught in many American drama schools dedicates too much time to:

> [h]elping actors deal with the fear of performance…it's telling them not to let the anxiety show. People who don't have acting training have coping mechanisms but they have them from life. I'm interested in the different ways that the people cope with the thing I'm asking them to do.[3]

The effect of this approach has been to present apparently vulnerable figures on stage; figures stripped of artifice and pretension. For the critic Sarah Hemming, both the performers *and* characters' "sense of vulnerability" is deeply affecting; she suggests that their emotional engagement is "raw" as if "they have lost a layer of skin."[4] The moments of awkwardness are subtle, so that the audience is often unsure as to whether the director was aware of, or in control of, the shortcomings of the actors' performance. At times the productions appear unfinished, as if the actors are showing a "walk-through" version of their play or as if they are gesturing towards an equivocation of their "big scene" rather than showing it in full. The journalist Wayne Alan Brenner reported overhearing an audience member say, "It's kind of like really *bad* acting, but *on purpose*."[5] Elsewhere I have referred to this level of finish as a "rehearsal aesthetic" — the glimpses of anxiety, nerves and difficulty, to which the audience are privy, break with the customary expectations in mainstream theatre, where actors will work to suppress signs of nerves or difficulty and show a honed, "finished" piece of work. Most importantly, conventional realism attempts to suppress signs of "rehearsal" and make invisible the many hours of labour and investment contributing to each finished production. For me, this rehearsal aesthetic suggests that Maxwell is aiming to capitalise on the risky, contingent nature of live performance in order to orient the audience towards the question, "Why are we here?" "What is it we all want from this play?"[6]

Maxwell's more recent works END OF REALITY (2006), ODE TO THE MAN WHO KNEELS (2007), PEOPLE WITHOUT HISTORY (2008), ADS (2010), DAS MAEDCHEN (2010) and NEUTRAL HERO (2011) demonstrate his desire to move away from a set "style" and experiment with a different set of approaches. ADS comprises a series of projected three-dimensional images (holograms) onto a focal point centre stage. About twenty participants "appear" on stage to describe a personal ideology or doctrine; some beliefs are long-held and deep-set, some are contingent and subject to change, some are orthodox, some esoteric, but all provide a foundation for the speaker's conviction that there is value and integrity to be found in all human endeavour. The scale of the images works to foster the illusion that the speakers are "present," but the relay of their voices over the PA system and the occasional flicker of the projection remind the audience that what they are watching is a recording. DAS MAEDCHEN, commissioned by Theatre Bonn in 2010, represented a departure from previous work because it experimented, for the first time, with physical theatre and dance. From a mixed ensemble of German and American actors (non-dancers), the performers were invited to respond spontaneously through movement and dance to the lines of the play projected on the screen above and behind them. For company members such as Sibyl Kempson this new approach demanded that she "let go" of any "preconceived experiences" about Maxwell's text and instead, "explor[ed] it new everytime."[7] Maxwell has stated that he is keen to keep changing direction, to keep working with new collaborators and keep learning. He is resistant to his work being described in terms of a recognizable "style" or "trademark," finding this shorthand designation "condescending."[8] Jim Fletcher, a long-term Maxwell collaborator has described the experience of working with Maxwell as being "in a boat." He suggests that:

> Rich is moving on, as he has been since I've known him. I don't usually know where we're going but I know where we are and what direction we're pointing in. Let's say you're in a boat, you know where you are?[9]

Maxwell's repeated change in direction has resulted, for me, in much confusion. Despite having followed his work since 2001, I am regularly confounded by the new work I encounter; just as I think I have "got it," that I have a coherent overview of what he is about and how he experiments with theatrical form, he presents something which is a dramatic departure from what went before. I consider that **THE END OF REALITY, PEOPLE WITHOUT HISTORY, ODE TO THE MAN WHO KNEELS** and **NEUTRAL HERO** are all pieces that have represented a deliberate departure, a marked shift in direction; they are also pieces, which despite their beauty, do not lend up their "meaning" easily. My attempts to theorise his work have included a determination to read his work as "post-humanist" — as critical of the illusion of the self-contained subject born with equal opportunity and an equal sense of agency. However, his recent work with "archetypes" in **NEUTRAL HERO** and **DAS MAEDCHEN** is theoretically at odds with a post-humanist reading.

Archetypes suggest a universality of experience across time and cultures and work to sublimate difference. Maxwell's work is so specific to American masculinity I find it difficult to marry this new approach with my drive to read his work as resisting the illusion of a universal subject.

Until recently I have understood his work to be a critique of individualism and the centrality of the myth of individualism to developed capitalist countries. This interpretation is informed by Maxwell's repeated reference to America, American culture and use of American vernacular. Myths of freedom and individualism underpin the popular conception of the American Dream, a philosophy characterising the sense of limitless optimism experienced by generations of American immigrants and settlers. Maxwell strikes me as having a deep affection for his country, but also as being driven by a desire to critique the illusion of equal opportunity and the capitalist drive to exploit its workers for minimum wage. The "heroes" of Maxwell's plays tend to be working class men from unconventional backgrounds. Despite their best intentions to succeed, to overcome all obstacles, their plans to move on are repeatedly stymied by a lack of education, an inability to speak rationally, the inability to recover from heartbreak. Even when his characters appear to be working towards therapeutic "closure" by sharing their feelings, they experience no comfort or relief. As the ensemble sings in **ODE TO THE MAN WHO KNEELS**, the best they can do is "endure". I have identified this critique of individualism in Maxwell's early experiments with neutrality—by setting out to relieve his actors of the burden of "emoting," Maxwell is refusing to create a distinction between actor and character; refusing to permit the actor to prioritise the fictional scenario over the reality of the performance. This approach strikes me as an effective way to undermine the individualistic ideology of Method Acting. By insisting his actors focus upon the immediate conditions of performance rather than an absent fictional "elsewhere," Maxwell ensures that his actors continue to "key into" one another and identify as a collective rather than a collection of individualistic virtuoso performers. David Krasner sees the refusal of the "higher, transcendent reality" associated with method-informed acting as problematic — for him:

> Determinists subordinate any seeming higher transcendent reality to the status of illusion. Actors' inquiry into things spiritual is futile once they accept their own material presence, they are given over to what David Mamet calls "the actual courage of the actor," a courage that when "coupled with the lines of the playwright [creates] the illusion of character." Actors cease to graft their individuality onto the role and accept their position as ÜBERMARIONETTES.[10]

I think that it is precisely Maxwell's intention to foreground the actor's material presence, to foreground their nerves and the difficulty of speaking in public so that their status as "übermarionettes," that is, as subjects compelled by wider social forces to behave in a certain way, becomes evident. Tim Etchells, Artistic Director of Forced Entertainment, has spoken of the live medium of theatre as one fraught with difficulty. He described it as an "economy of humiliation" in which, "you betray yourself, you show more than you wish to, you stumble, you slip. It's simple: you stand there and you fail."[11] In Maxwell's work, as in that of Forced Entertainment, acting works as a metaphor for the activity of communicating and interacting in everyday life: it is a high-risk activity, one that is particularly onerous for those unschooled in the rhetoric of dissembling and pretence.

Although these ideas may still have some currency when applied to **NEUTRAL HERO**, the presence of archetypes does not sit easily with a post-humanist critique. The anti-heroes of Maxwell's previous work have worked to resist the myth of individualism, the notion that an individual can transcend his or her origins to realise their goals. However, NEUTRAL HERO is informed by the "hero-paradigm" discussed by Joseph Campbell in *The Hero With A Thousand Faces*.[12] Campbell argues that a diversity of myths collected from across the globe evidence a common structure, and can be understood in terms of a "monomyth". Maxwell stated that as a starting point for the piece he began to "imagine the paradigm without any cultural identity."[13] Maxwell has recognised the paradox this proposition represents and has explained that any frustration caused by the proposition of a generalised American experience is intentional:

> I wanted to strip these tales bare in order to touch on something deeply rooted in them. There is a paradox in the idea of bringing something neutral to the stage. It's irritating and provocative. At the same time, I realise that I am an American. The actors are American and express themselves in English. And that is another paradox — neutral and American. What is neutral? That raises the question, What is not neutral? And that places us just where I want, in a state of suspension, of frustrating suspension.[14]

For me, the denial of the importance of cultural identity is at odds with my understanding of Maxwell's previous work. The particularity of its references to specific fast food chains, brand-named shoes, American football and baseball locate the work firmly within American culture: an understanding of the importance of cultural identity and the particularity of that experience to America seems crucial to this work. The promotional booklet for Kunstenfestivaldesarts 2011 reveals that the show was originally promoted with the subtitle, "American is the Amateur." This subtitle compounds the sense that Maxwell is using a narrative about an individual to act as a metaphor for a wider society beyond the confines of the world of the hero. Although, in the past, I have inferred a critique of American culture generally in his work, the apparent affection Maxwell has for his characters, and the

Neutral Hero — Photo: Almudena Crespo

differing points of view presented, has prevented me from necessarily reading his work as metonymic. When quizzed about this subtitle Maxwell refers to American history—appearing to imply that America could be seen as the amateur in its attempts to ape the sovereign British powers from which it sought independence. He has stated that "American is the Amateur" is a phrase that:

> ...guides me, like a beacon. [...] I got there by recognising that we are Americans, examining the identity of this country, its historical foundations. [...] We wanted to make money like the British, but didn't want to be dictated to by their king, we wanted our own status. That is fundamental for understanding the "amateur." All this seems to be denied today. See what's happening in entertainment, where what matters is the virtuosity, the professionalism, the quality. It is veritable privatisation, a dispossession of our collective experience. This phrase "American is the Amateur" is an overt challenge to that.[15]

This speech offers several insights to help me out of my confusion. Here I ascertain that Maxwell's intention is to question the value of monomyths as representations of "collective experience" and problematise the denigration of amateur performance when this form could provide a more authentic voice and an opportunity for the collective to take ownership of the story.

NEUTRAL HERO presents us with an apparently amateur ensemble of performers who occupy the stage in order to share in the narrative of the "hero" (played by Alex Delinois). The ensemble is chiefly made up of untrained actors, who, although perhaps new to the stage, are extremely proficient musicians. From the ensemble, who sit in a large semi-circle, key figures emerge: a mother, a father, a son and the hero's wife—his "goddess". Through a combination of song and prose we learn that the son suffered as a result of his father

People Without History — Photo: Michael Schmelling

being absent and witness his journey to reconcile himself both with his father and the fact of his absence. The son embarks upon a journey but fails to resist temptation: he is unfaithful and commits crimes. It is unclear whether he returns with a "boon"; his grateful cries of "yeah!" do not suggest he has been bestowed with the gift of great insight, but he does appear to be re-accepted into his community by an elderly figure that reassures him:

> I'm here, no matter what. You're doing the right thing. Let them punish you, let them cause you extreme pain on your person; let them set you on fire. I'm here to tell you it doesn't matter what happens, you are in the right room.[16]

Although the incorporation of archetypes strikes me as a new departure, much of the performance bears a close relation to previous Maxwell productions. House lights remain illuminated, the performers are seated on functional furniture customarily associated with municipal buildings, the actors are conservative in their gestures and movement and they adopt an uninflected tone when delivering lines. For Dan Ruppel, "the troupe intoned their lines like struggling readers, students who demonstrate sufficient grasp of the phonetic system to pronounce words, but not to give them meaningful inflection."[17] Although for some critics the lack of inflection was off-putting[18] many found much to appreciate in the minimalism of Maxwell's direction. Avia Moore wrote:

> ...I started to feel that [the monotone delivery] was actually creating a space for unusual subtleties. When every line is approached flatly, a small look and a gentle question mark are suddenly very touching. A slight waver and a moment of eye contact become more intensely emotional because they are so rare.[19]

Although Maxwell may shy away from designating his performers "amateurs", he clearly values the potential of amateurism to undermine, or resist, the discourse of mastery and achievement associated with virtuosity. In interview with Jean-Louis Perrier he conceives of the American President Barack Obama as "*amateur* in a positive way," because he is seen to lack the established background in politics that Republican politicians (and many Democrats) expect from a US President. Despite the presence of archetypes, my sense is that Maxwell continues to champion subaltern subjects in this production, the plight of the eponymous "neutral hero" in this piece has been deliberately formulated in resistance to our understanding of the archetypal hero as a young, white, privileged, middle-class male. The eponymous hero is played by Alex Delinois, a black male performer. Witnessing his downfall and his subsequent restitution acted as a sober reminder of the disadvantages many young African Americans continue to face and the scarcity of black faces on the Western stage. At the close of the play the hero's mother delivers the line, "Thank you for listening. Not a lot of people care"—another reminder that the plight of young African Americans, until recently, has been marginalised and rarely connected to the responsibilities of the wider community. Perrier, in his interview, inadvertently offends Maxwell by suggesting that, "these characters are different from us, by way of their social status, their behaviour, their language—the public should not be open to them; is this not a way for you to…drive the public to accept them?" Maxwell responds that he feels:

> [C]onstrained by this way of thinking; I have the impression that you respond like this, not because what you see on stage is inconsistent with life, but because it doesn't concord with what you are used to seeing on stage. When I go to other theatres, I see exactly what you describe: strange people, acting strangely, who are not how people are.[20]

It would appear that Maxwell is keen to take back control of the "collective experience" by placing marginalised subjects and their experience centre stage. He also encourages subaltern subjects to eschew the ideology of virtuosity—instead he suggests they go on stage and share their experience in a way that renders their disadvantage, their lack of privilege clear. Many critics and commentators draw attention to the use of amateurs in Maxwell's work without considering the function they may serve in capturing something of the sense of what it means to be and remain marginalised because one has not been inculcated with a sense of entitlement or schooled in the skills of self-presentation. Promotional copy for Neutral Hero suggests that the small-town occupants sing "with the disarming sincerity of the guileless," indicating, for me, that Maxwell equates the amateur (one without an established background in the discipline) with a lack of guile—without "insidious cunning, crafty or artful duplicity."[21] One of the questions Maxwell wanted to raise in employing an archetypal hero was, "Can your hero be black? Can it be a woman?"[22] Maxwell has recognised the continuing influence of the American Civil War as "a wound that is still open today" and is frustrated by the failure of his countrymen to see that past resentment still runs deep. I'm relieved to see the potential to find a critique of Humanism and Humanist values still runs through Neutral Hero. It seems that Maxwell's decision to employ archetypes opens up the problems associated with a collective imagining of archetypal heroes as white middle class men. The founding fathers were not neutral heroes; they were privileged, "aristocratic" and "homogenous"; their heroic status was predicated upon their ability to represent the universal subject. The "black" neutral hero in Maxwell's piece is an unresolvable paradox with the potential to puncture the illusion of self-determination and Individual freedom.

So, for those who dismiss Maxwell's recent work as "aggravating," "condescending,"[23] "preachy" or "without warmth"[24] I would beseech them to consider the efficacy of his actors' awkwardness and to think more carefully about the intention behind his desire to question virtuosity. Maxwell manifests a profound fondness for his country, showing affection for working people and the mundane routine of everyday American life. However he also questions the normalisation of individualism—by interrogating the role and function of local and national community he makes clear the influence of mainstream ideology in determining who "gets ahead." His characters are blue-collar workers, support staff, cowboys or working class citizens attempting to make sense of a rapidly changing environment. They try to reconcile their own inertia with the myth of freedom and equal opportunity promoted as part of The American Dream. Their inability to make sense of the contradictions they experience provides a vital counterpoint to the mainstream ideology of liberal capitalism promulgated internationally by the slick "professional" aesthetic of Hollywood films and TV exports.

1. Wessendorf, Markus "The (Un)Settled Space of Richard Maxwell's House" in *Modern Drama 44* (4) (Ontario: University of Toronto Press, 2001) p.455.
2. For a more developed discussion of Maxwell's work with trained and untrained actors see Gorman, Sarah "Bad Acting on Purpose" in *The Theatre of Richard Maxwell and the New York City Players* (New York: Routledge, 2011) pp.30–49.
3. Ellis, Samantha "Numb and Number" The Guardian 2nd March, 2005. Available at: http://www.guardian.co.uk/stage/2005/mar/02/theatre4. Accessed 17 November, 2005.
4. Hemming, Sarah "More than words: the Silent Blend in Maxwell's House" Financial Times, 7 March, 2005. http://www.ft.com/cms/s/2/69a15934-8ead-11d9-8aae00000e2511c8.html#axzz1X5NLpVDc, accessed 17 November, 2005.
5. Brenner, Wayne Alan "Drummer Wanted: Richard Maxwell" The Austin Chronicle 2003:1 http://www.austinchronicle.com/issues/dispach/2003—01—1/arts_exhibitionism5.html. Accessed 15 July, 2003.
6. I discuss Maxwell's 'rehearsal aesthetic' in "Concert Hall Slash Sports Facility: The Anthropological Space of Richard Maxwell's Theatre"—Chapter 5 of *The Theatre of Richard Maxwell and the New York City Players* (London: Routledge, 2011) p.91–116.
7. Talk-Back with New York City Players at Kammerspeilhaus, Bad Godesburg, 27 June, 2010.
8. Gorman, Sarah "Refusing Shorthand: Richard Maxwell" in *Contemporary Theatre Review*, Vol. 17(2) (Chur, Switzerland: Harwood Academic, 2007) pp.235–241.
9. Kunstenfestivaldesarts 011 programme *Neutral Hero*, May 2011, p.4.
10. Krasner, David *Method Acting Reconsidered: Theory, Practice, Future* (Hampshire: Macmillan Press, 2000) p.20
11. Etchells, Tim *Presentation at Live Culture Event*, Tate Modern, London. 29 March, 2003.

12. Campbell, Joseph *The Hero With A Thousand Faces* (New York: Pantheon Books, 1949).
13. Ibid.
14. Press Kit *Neutral Hero*, Festival Transamériques 2011, p.3 http://www.fta.qc.ca/sites/fta.qc.ca/.../press_kit_fta_2011_neutral_hero_eng.pdf, accessed 1 September, 2011.
15. Kunstenfestivaldesarts 011 programme—*Neutral Hero*, p.23. Original emphasis.
16. *Neutral Hero* script, unpublished.
17. Ruppel, Dan "Neutralizing the Burden of Emotion" *Rover: Montreal Arts Uncovered* http://roverarts.com/2011/06/violent-beauty-beautiful-violence/, accessed 1 September, 2011.
18. Yosi Wanunu described it as 'Beckett without the poetry' in *The American Myth: Neutral Hero by Richard Maxwell*, Corpus, http://www.corpusweb.net/the-american-myth.html, accessed 1 September, 2011.
19. Moore, Avia "'Gardenia' from Les Ballet C de la B and Richard Maxwell's 'Neutral Hero'" *Culturebot* http://culturebot.net/2011/06/10810/gardenia-from-les-ballet-c-de-la-b-and-richard-maxwell%E2%80%99s-neutral-hero/, accessed 1 September, 2011.
20. Kunstenfestivaldesarts 2011 promotional leaflet: *Neutral Hero*, p 25
21. *Collins English Dictionary*, (Glasgow: Harper Collins, 1991).
22. Interview with Playwright 1 December, 2010.
23. Ruppel, Dan "Neutralizing the Burden of Emotion" *Rover: Montreal Arts Uncovered* 6 June, 2011 http://roverarts.com/2011/06/violent-beauty-beautiful-violence/, accessed 1 September, 2011.
24. Wanunu, Yosi *The American Myth: Neutral Hero by Richard Maxwell* Corpus, http://www.corpusweb.net/the-american-myth.html, accessed 1 September, 2011.

ESSAY 10

CULTIVATED CHAOS: MOMENT SPECIFIC DRAMATURGY

SODJA ZUPANC LOTKER

DIP INTO THE UNKNOWN

In 2008, the Hungarian theatre director Árpád Schilling changed the name of the Krétakör Színház to simply Krétakör, removing the word színház (theatre) from its title and disbanding the company of actors. At that time the company was functioning as an independent entity (a rare achievement in Eastern Europe) and winning awards such as the Grand Prix at Belgrade's BITEF international theatre festival, the first prize of festival Premiers Plans d'Angers and the New Theatrical Realities award at the Europe Theatre Prize. Krétakör Színház made productions of "classic" plays—Brecht's **BAAL** (1998), Molnár's **LILIOM** (2001), Georg Büchner's **LEONCE AND LENA** (2002), Moliere's **MISANTHROPE** (2004) and Ibsen's **PEER GYNT** (2005) which is what we in Central and Eastern Europe tend to call "director's theatre"—where the director is the central motor in the creation of new interpretations of plays and autonomously creates "added value" to the playwright's text. Krétakör Színház was favoured even among those not partial to traditional drama because Árpád Schilling used a variety of theatrical tools, incorporating visual elements, singing or movement as well as explorations of the theatre space that broke down the traditional audience-performance relationship.

Now imagine this: an installation of cars standing on their heads, or filled up with toys, in parking lots, streets and squares around the city of Budapest; a photographic slide show installation (in an industrial space) of a long-haired, bearded man, naked, breaking a wall in his living room; half-naked men singing and dancing in a real shower in real time; a miniature, traditional "red velvet" theatre behind which a husband and wife argue in their big living room; a video diary of a pregnant woman's verbal hallucinations; people sitting in their living room watching the snow of a non-functioning TV; pregnant women singing a lullaby in a swimming-pool; (real) teenagers having a birthday party; a dance ball for senior citizens...as well a picnic along the 9th district of Budapest. All of this took place in **APOLOGY OF AN ESCAPOLOGIST** (2008), the first project by the "new" Krétakör.

All together this sounds like "something different" for theatre—and it is. In **ESCAPOLOGIST** there was no plot, no narrative—hardly any of the "characters" reappeared through different fragments. Some parts involved installations without performers, others used video, others personal diary, community theatre and site specific performance.

Fragmentation is one of the fundamental dramaturgical strategies of contemporary performance, but here the audiences had to follow this performance-project for about eight weeks in more than six found spaces around Budapest through a series of more than twenty events and two installations: an experience I would call *total fragmentation*. *Total fragmentation* is the separation not only of scenes, ideas and themes but of the performance itself into different spaces, places, times, as well as a fragmentation of the audience, since not all audience members went to every event and could see them in any order. What is interesting is not so much the confusion this *total fragmentation* created among audiences and theatre critics, as well as a crisis it has created around the company—the interesting thing is how much it makes sense.

It is worth considering Árpád Schilling, a person who at that point was about to become a father for the first time. The idea of a child completely changed the way he perceived things, as if the whole world had blown up right in front of his face into small fragments. The central director's point of view—in which the director is responsible for all the answers, the unifier of all goals and the creator of a central experience for the audience—was no longer enough. The new life, the child, a person one has responsibility for without having any idea of their perspective, shifts the point of view into the unknown. The world has changed into something much bigger than oneself. The experience was no longer unified.

With his baby, Árpád Schilling, the "escapologist", has willingly, consciously, conceptually dipped into the total unknown.

MULTIPLE EXPERIENCE

The case of Árpád Schilling's **ESCAPOLOGIST** is a good example of the decentralisation of meaning in contemporary performance. This decentralisation is caused by the realisation that there are "others" present. Seeing the multiplicity of meaning we understand that there is a certain "chaos of meaning". Seen through the eyes of others the world becomes too complex to seize.

Schilling's "baby" summons to mind theories such as "encounter with the other"; gender theories and the notion of multiple gaze; as well as the overall understanding that all meaning is not "uniform" but constructed by each specific person in a specific space at a specific time. All of the ideas are significant for contemporary performance and have influenced its dramaturgy,[1] changing the structure traditionally centred on a story, one plot to address the multiplicity of meanings, readings and positions. The traditional coherent plot of a "well made" theatre play was atomised into a script with fragments as the main dramaturgical building blocks. Throughout the twentieth century this artistic strategy of fragmentary dramaturgy has been used by playwrights such as Gertrude Stein, Heiner Mueller and Sarah Kane or directors such as Robert Wilson and Richard Foreman.

Throughout the seven sub-events of **APOLOGY OF AN ESCAPOLOGIST**, the baby's environment is explored from different points of view and in different points in time and space, even portraying past and future. These fragments each had their own theme and included the exploration of the city environment, the inner questioning of the father and the psychophysical problems of the mother's pregnancy, as well as depictions of life among different generations in Hungary expressed through community theatre.

But with **APOLOGY OF AN ESCAPOLOGIST** the decentralisation happened on multiple levels: on the level of the script, the story—but also within the process of its making. It is an example of recent developments in performance where the decentralisation goes beyond the script, the dramaturgical, aesthetical decentralisation, to also consider the decentralisation of process, tools and experience—that of operations.

The change of an operational mode is one of the main aspects of Krétakör Theatre's transformation into Krétakör, stemming from Árpád Schilling's need to decentralise his own self, the persona of the director. **ESCAPOLOGIST** was the first step towards collaborative creation, a project devised with media artists, musicians and other directors as a means to decentralise the process of theatre making. The collaborative systems of creation are in constant development and are one of the central questions of the new Krétakör. In the Crisis Trilogy[1] project created during 2010/11, Árpád Schilling purposely shared the project with young inexperienced artists from the company who each directed separate parts. Krétakör's decentralised collaboration subscribes to the devised theatre's "process for creating performance from scratch, by the group, without pre-existing script,"[2] where the devising stands both for the collaborative creation of the whole team as well as for the creation of the script through the rehearsal process. Thus, both on the level of process and that of the product, the multiple experiences of the creators are represented.

The audience's experience in contemporary theatre is decentralised, too. It offers a possibility of multiplicity of experiences — "an anarchic way of viewing" performance as director and theorist Alan Read would say. It is represented by the fragmentation of the performance script, in which the audiences' brains, their mental instinct, connects with and makes sense of the fragmentary composition. In *total fragmentation* this sense of decentralisation is reinforced by the fragmentation of the performance itself into multiple places and times.

The multiplication of experience is a distinctive feature of the work of Italian company Fanny and Alexander, for instance. Its performance piece TEL (2011) is divided into two events taking place in two different cities at exactly the same time, where two performers have a dialogue by phone. The text, the music, the choreography are one and the same performed by a male actor in one place and a female actor in the other place. The audience is divided in two, watching a story of T. E. Lawrence, himself divided into both commander and subordinate in a story of war and politics, where the points of view are easily shifted.

In Krétakör's APOLOGY OF AN ESCAPOLOGIST each audience member had a choice of seeing the performance in their own arrangement, watching any number of parts, in any order. In CEMETERY, the installation of cars, or GAP, the photographic slide-show installation, the audience also had free movement within the space and could create their own dramaturgy within it. Here audiences becomes independent temporally and spatially and thus responsible for their own dramaturgical composition. The system of devising, of sharing the creative process with the collaborators as well as the audiences, is at the core of the artistic concept for Árpád Schilling's new Krétakör, trying to grasp the multiple-gazes beyond his own reach.

MOMENT SPECIFIC DRAMATURGY

The *total fragmentation* on multiple levels takes into consideration the multiplicity of reality—the multiple experiences of multiple creators as well as multiple experiences of the audiences, here regarded as co-creators. The decentralisation of meaning in *total fragmentation* leads to independence of individual units of the script, their "emancipation" from the whole, where each unit gains its own space time, has its own logic, and stands for a world of its own. This phenomenon can be called *moment specific dramaturgy*, a method of performance composition where these units, whether they are moments, or performers/characters, or scenes, gain their independence. They become multiple centres, the carriers of dramaturgy, and are grounded in individual content. Each dramaturgical unit has its own place—in space and time, as well as its own method, each made with a specific tool, thus multiplying the languages within performance.

DECENTRALISATION OF LANGUAGE

In performances created by companies such as Fanny and Alexander, Gob Squad, Superamas, Needcompany, or Cia Dani Lima—the multiplication of language is highly visible. Each part within the fragmentary script is created with different tools—media, painting, text, movement, toys, quotes, animals, songs—in order to create very precise concepts, moods, ideas.

Just looking at the list of works by Gob Squad, the German/British theatre company which has existed since 1992, and how they "label" their performances will give us a hint of the diversity of tools, genres and languages used, specific and different for each performance. The list includes: BEFORE YOUR VERY EYES (2011)—a "performance with children"; KING KONG CLUB (2005) an "interactive film event"; WHO ARE YOU WEARING? (2004) "durational performance"; THE GREAT OUTDOORS (2002) "a multimedia performance". That list also includes,

Apology of an Escapologist
Photo: Dávid Udvardy

"a karaoke casting show"; a "multi-perspective film event"; "an online performance"; "an internet radio docu-soap"; "an interactive party performance"; "a live radio performance"; "a video installation" and extends to "half group therapy, half performance nightmare" and "a real uprising staged for the cameras", as well as "a live film with bad coffee, nervous breakdown, wild parties and modern hairstyles".

The practice of using specific, discrete tools to create unique moments in performance can also be found in the work of the French-Austrian company Superamas. The individual scenes of **THE BIG 3RD EPISODE** (2006) include a rock concert, a film, a soap opera and a philosophical discussion to suggest that the face of happiness is only a face; a superficial representation of its impossibility.

In the work of Jan Lauwers's Belgian group, Needcompany, the specificity of tools and language can be found on a different dramaturgical level: the level of character. In **ISABELLA'S ROOM** (2004), the titular character's foster parents speak different languages — Flemish for her mother, French for her father — while her true father, the Desert Prince, uses the language of contemporary dance. This creates a set of independent individuals, "portraits" of people who are so separate, so different, so mutually incomprehensible, that the harmony between them stands for the miracle of life itself.

In the dramaturgy of decentralised, fragmentary performance *specific* tends to be a crucial word. The multiplicity of experiences, of points in time and space, of viewpoints between creators, "characters" and audiences, is so expansive that the dramaturgy has to be rooted in something precise.

This is something I came to realise while working as a dramaturg on **STRATEGY NO. 1: IN BETWEEN** (2005), a performance by the Brazilian choreographer Dani Lima, which explored the multiplicity of experience in even a simple encounter, and the pull between fact and fiction within a co-existence of relationship between two human beings. **STRATEGY NO. 1: IN BETWEEN** took place between one performer and one audience member in an apartment, and it consisted of a series of units whose order was to be chosen by the spectator. The units were miniature replications of encounters between two people, and represented a variety of experiences.

While talking about individual strategies for each unit we tended to look for a "best" approach, a specific form for every encounter. One scene, addressing the pool of one's memory and the impossibility of completely sharing it with others, was represented by a box full of buttons from which the audience member had to choose only one to take as a gift. A scene of abuse was enacted by the audience member laying on the floor while the performer lay on them and softly whispered in their ear a story of violence. Within these units the performer and audience member also recited, danced, made drawings and took photographs, as though each new tool, mode, genre or form represented another perspective. During work on **STRATEGY NO. 1** I realised that these pieces do not refer to the medium anymore, to the fragmentation itself anymore, but that the "message" freely chooses its specific tool.

The focus of 20th Century theatre gradually moved from a general sense of theatre craft—the written play and the enacting of it—through the innovations of directors such as Stanislavsky or later Grotowski, who created their own specific languages, tools and ways of working. Different directors focused on developing a specific craft, such as a method of acting, directing and research, or a particular aesthetic. The decentralised performances of recent decades is using a multiplicity of such languages, which leads to *extremely specific tools for individual dramaturgical units* within a performance, and thus productions become trans-disciplinary, using many tools and many (often conflicting) aesthetics.

The latest project by Krétakör, for instance, the **CRISIS TRILOGY** (2011), is an extreme experimentation in ways of expressing a multiplicity of performative languages—it is a photo exhibition that becomes community theatre that becomes a film that becomes an opera that becomes a theatre game and that could as easily have been a street intervention, a circus, slide show projection, an installation…

Because of its experimentation with languages and tools, Krétakör is not recognised (and does not want to be recognised) as a theatre anymore. This multiplication of language has proved crucial for Krétakör, with consequences that go beyond the dramaturgical: it has led to problems with the vital state funding. The use of different languages also causes problems between Krétakör and theatre critics. Most of the theatre critics simply ignore the new work of Krétakör, some bluntly criticising their work for not being theatre, while only one Hungarian critic has admitted in an article to not having the tools, knowledge and terminology to write about the work.

I don't blame these critics: it is problematic to critically read performances of open fragmentary dramaturgy with decentralised meaning, because these performances are created for the "anarchic way of viewing," and not one clear central critical eye. They are built in decentralised ways by many people together, and do not represent one central director's point of view—not to mention the multi-disciplinary languages they involve which most critics are not equipped to address.

DECENTRALISED COMPOSITION

The dramaturgical composition of decentralised *total fragmentation* is also challenging. For each performance, and very often from moment to moment within the performance, a different strategy, tool or medium is required—as a specific, precise solution for a specific dramaturgical unit. Facing the chaos of possibilities in the decentralised theatre of multiple experiences, its individual units are explored deeper, rooted to specific languages, strengthened individually. The overall performance does not represent a whole anymore, one story, one point of view, one truth—but each moment carries its own individual "truth".

These specific "solutions" to individual dramaturgical moments are "one off" solutions for a specific performance, artist, character, moment, point of view, or point in time and space. But though they are seemingly random they are carefully chosen to be extremely precise in creating texture, colour, taste. A series of such units, especially if grounded in different space and time as is the case in *total fragmentation*, represents a certain chaos, especially if we are thinking from the point of view of traditional theatre, where dramaturgy, script and the flow of performance is based on transformations of characters and the situations between them, united within one aesthetic.

The structure of *total fragmentation* performances needs to be looked at from the standpoint of visual or musical composition so that its seeming chaos gains different dimensions. In this sense contemporary theatre has not lost its dramatic aspect—the drama still happens within the composition of relationships of the units; in their clashing, contrasts, harmony. If each unit has its own integrity, language, colour, aesthetic, dynamic and theme the spatio-temporal composition gains incredible possibilities in combination within the performance. Spatial and temporal dynamics become the core of the dramatic composition in this era of fragmentary dramaturgy, of multiple-experience.

Moment specific dramaturgy, in its use of multiple languages and tools, represents a cultivation of chaos, where chaos is contained in the specificity of individual units and the spatio-temporal composition between them. It does not represent one solution but a series of options, where each unit carries its own "momentary" truth. Paradoxically, chaos can be used to compose.

MULTIPLE EVENTS OF TOTAL FRAGMENTATION

The need to express a multiplicity of experiences through *total fragmentation* in which each unit has such independence, a momentary truth, to an extant of autonomy of space, time and language, replaces individual performances with a series of events. Krétakör's **APOLOGY OF AN ESCAPOLOGIST** included four dramaturgical parts that took place in seven places over two months, then adjourned to **ANALOGY OF AN ESCAPOLOGIST**, a series of four concerts which took place during 2009/2010, and an **APOLOGY OF AN ESCAPOLOGIST** DVD, that is an art project in itself and not a mere documentation of a performance.

Performances of Italian company Fanny and Alexander also come in "groups". The above mentioned performance **TEL** is part of **LAWRENCE PROJECT** exploring the historical figure, ideas of distance, war and Arab revolt. The **LAWRENCE PROJECT** consists of: **TEL**: a show for two actors; **338171 TEL**: a radio drama (2011); and **REVOLT IN THE DESERT**: a show for ten performers and five writers (2013). The work of Fanny and Alexander, as well as other Italian companies such as Motus, can be defined as research opus rather than performances, a series of sub-events centred on one theme but exploring a multiplicity of different points of view. Motus's **SYRMA ANTIGONES** (2009) explored the ancient tragedy Antigone in relation to the 2008 street demonstrations in Greece, while questioning revolution in today's society. This consisted of four main performances which later resolved into a live interview between Motus and Judith Malina of New York's The Living Theatre called **THE PLOT IS THE REVOLUTION** (2011).

Fanny and Alexander's project O – Z (2008–2010), explored the journey theme from **THE WIZARD OF OZ** story, wondering "is it possible to see without being in the place we are trying to see?" (Lagani, Angelis 2010:10).[4] O – Z includes eight parts, including stage performance, opera, installations, as well as a book that is an art project in its own right. It is emblematic of total fragmentation, whose artists deal in multiplicity of experiences, represented by deeply considered, diverse sub-events. These are a series of units, of events, of new languages, that represent different positions along the journey towards the place where one is not, but which we are trying to see.

1. In this text I use the word dramaturgy to mean the spatio-temporal composition of performance, and not the professional role within performance making.
2. *The Crisis Trilogy* is developed by Krétakör in cooperation with Prague Quadrennial of Performance Design and Space, Bayerische Staatsoper, Munich and Trafó—House of Contemporary Arts, Budapest in 2009/2011.
3. From *Devising Performance: a Critical History*. Edited by Heddon, Deirdre and Milling, Jane (Basingstoke, England: Palgrave Macmillan, 2006) p3
4. From *Fanny and Alexander* "Atlange di un viaggio teatrele/Atlas of a Theatre Journey" (Ubulibri, 2010).

Apology of an Escapologist, Cemetery
Photo: Dávid Udvardy

ESSAY 11

THE PEOPLE IN THE ROOM: A KIND OF CONVERSATION ABOUT QUARANTINE

QUARANTINE

Like many artists, we are hesitant to make definitive statements about our work. Even that sentence feels too rigid. We're certain that uncertainty suits us and the way we see the world. Quarantine's work embraces ambiguity, serious intentions, fragile doubts — and is driven by asking questions for which we have no answers. Writing this down can appear to deal in absolutes. The concern is that what we think we might be saying might not be what you're hearing. Dialogue is always what makes work interesting.

We have asked others to answer some questions about our work to allow a variety of voices to explore the possibilities of our approach to making theatre. We have collected a group of people together, bound by these pages, to begin a conversation. First though, some questions that we need to answer ourselves:

WHO ARE WE?

Quarantine was set up in 1998 by directors Richard Gregory and Renny O'Shea and designer Simon Banham. Beyond this core group we work with a shifting constellation of collaborators, always saying that each piece of work is by Quarantine, rather than singling out an individual artist. Quarantine is the umbrella we all shelter under.

HOW DO WE BEGIN?

…with the people in the room. Where they come from varies, but material is found in their personal histories, beliefs and possibilities. We are as curious about who people are as about what they can do, as interested in collaborating with experienced performers and artists as we are with people who haven't done anything like this before. People in Quarantine's work are not interpreters, but individuals, each with their own story. We're drawn to working with those whose

A KIND OF CONVERSATION...

voice is rarely heard. Our process is lengthy and discursive, a mix of rigorous practice, seemingly aimless conversation and moments that somehow stick, apparently discovered by accident.

WHAT ARE WE MAKING?

...something for the people who enter the room later—the audience. We question the mundane and familiar in the context of a theatrical event, interrogating the social/cultural/political/aesthetic act of being in a theatre, to provoke questions about what is happening in that space, and then perhaps/hopefully beyond the walls of the room.

We're interested in that which is invisible to us...What happens beyond that point where an audience connects with a performance? What happens inside the venue—and what happens afterwards? We're not the first to say it, but the important thing is: what remains?

Perhaps all that this throws up is another series of questions: there is never a resolution. From rehearsal rooms, conferences, cafés and park benches, here are a collection of answers from some of the people with whom we have shared rooms. We've edited and selected from their responses and biographies, sometimes brutally. We hope that you can hear their voices in the conversation...

THE CONTRIBUTORS

HB   We met Harley Bartles in a youth club in Newton Heath, Manchester. He was a performer (alongside six other young men) in our 2004 dirty ballet **WHITE TRASH** and later toured the world with the Belgian theatre company Victoria (now Campo). He currently works as an Account Manager in the Promotional Merchandise industry. Harley failed his GCSE drama.

MB   Michael Brady's sister used to share a house with Richard Gregory. They first met when Michael was 16 and have been good friends ever since. He is now a senior lecturer in philosophy at Glasgow University and asked us difficult questions about our values in the process of **MAKE-BELIEVE** (2009) and about the nature of hope for **ENTITLED** (2011).

LD   Lesa Dryburgh was born in Salford, lives in Manchester and works across the UK with people and companies to develop business and profile. She has enjoyed Quarantine's work over the past decade and has recently worked with the company to explore digital communications. Lesa is a Clore Fellow.

FE   J. Fergus Evans saw **SUSAN & DARREN** (2006), our event with dancing made with a mother and son (see "DP" below) and met Renny when he was part of the At Home residency scheme at Contact, Manchester. He is a spoken word and performance artist, works as an Assessor for Arts Council England and is a certified Coach working with people in the arts.

LE   Lowri Evans was studying art in Manchester when she saw **WHITE TRASH**, and liked it so much she went back. Since then she has seen most of Quarantine's work and performed in Make-believe, including a mean air bass in our version of Guns n' Roses' "Paradise City." Lowri makes live art in Manchester.

MF   Matt Fenton saw **EAT EAT**, the meal-based performance made with refugees and asylum seekers, in Leicester in 2003. Having a soft spot for Belgium, he followed the project, reinvented as **RANTSOEN** (2004), to **VICTORIA** in Ghent, and has followed and programmed the company ever since. Previously Director of Nuffield Theatre Lancaster, Matt is now Director of Live at LICA (Lancaster Institute For The Contemporary Arts).

Susan & Darren — Photo: Simon Banham

EG Emma Gladstone is a Londoner, with a slow burning desire to live somewhere else. She danced for over 20 years before starting what her mother called "a proper job". Emma met Quarantine a few years ago and programmed SUSAN & DARREN at Sadler's Wells, where she is based. She co-commissioned ENTITLED.

GH Geraldine (Gerry) Harris introduces herself as Menopausal Professor of Theatre Studies at Lancaster University. She saw SUSAN & DARREN in 2006 which led her to meet Renny and Richard in Manchester and write an article about the piece for Performance Research 13 (4). She already knew Simon Banham.

SH Sonia Hughes first met Renny through an anti-deportation campaign in Manchester in the 1980s. Thirteen years later she met Richard and was drawn to stuff he said about honesty. She was the writer on SUSAN & DARREN, MAKE-BELIEVE and ENTITLED.

AK Adrian Kear is Professor of Theatre and Performance at Aberystwyth University, where Simon Banham also works as a Senior Lecturer. He moved to Wales in 2007, living for a while in Simon's barn. He has published widely on contemporary European theatre, philosophy and performance.

AL Annie Lloyd is an independent producer in Leeds and member of Compass Live Art consortium. She was Director of The Gallery and Studio Theatre at Leeds Met University where she nurtured new performance work for 18 years. Annie presented SUSAN & DARREN in Leeds and commissioned THE SOLDIER'S SONG, Quarantine's karaoke video installation made with currently serving British soldiers.

FM Florian Malzacher met Richard when they facilitated MAKE, an international theatre project in Ireland. He is co-programmer

Old People, Children and Animals
Photo: Simon Banham

of steirischer herbst festival in Graz and founding member of the independent curators' collective Unfriendly Takeover. His publications include books on Forced Entertainment and Rimini Protokoll and on curating performing arts.

DP Darren Pritchard was in Renny's first show at **CONTACT YOUTH THEATRE**, Manchester when he was 12. He has performed in our one-on-one piece in the dark, something a taxi driver in Liverpool said…(2001), the chaotic attempt to squeeze a city onto a stage, **GRACE** (2005) and continues to perform with his mum in **SUSAN & DARREN** (since 2006). He is Artistic Director of Company Fierce and Mr Pole Dance UK 2010.

SS1 Steve Slater lived near Richard in Derbyshire for 20 years but they never met. Steve commissioned Quarantine's first piece **SEE-SAW** which re-launched Tramway, Glasgow in 2000. **SEE-SAW** had 75 performers intermingled with the audience, who faced each other across 2 seating banks. He now runs his own company, Tactical A.U. and is a freelance Creative Producer, father and dog walker.

SS2 Swen Steinhauser met Richard and Renny at Piccadilly station, Manchester in 2007 for a chat about making theatre with non-performers. He took part in Quarantine's mentoring scheme and was dramaturg on **THE SLIGHTEST MOVEMENT**, an attempt to create a temporary community of strangers which the audience were paid to attend and **ENTITLED**. Swen is a theatre director, lecturer, curator and PhD student in Cultural Studies.

CT Cait Taylor is Renny's (younger) sister. She has seen almost all Quarantine's work—and work from Renny, Richard and Simon before Quarantine existed. She is a GP in Liverpool and a qualified acupuncturist.

MT Michael Trainor and Quarantine were neighbours in Manchester's Northern Quarter. He is an artist who makes work about mass consumerism and light (separately). He says, "If it is by Quarantine I go, I don't even look at what it is." He owns a building we always say we want to move into but never do.

SB/RG/RS Simon Banham, Richard Gregory and Renny O'Shea first worked together at Contact Theatre, Manchester in 1991. We've collaborated ever since. Simon lives in Wales. Richard and Renny live in England. Somehow we manage to keep talking.

…quite theatre-set-like sets with a highly calculated feel of the ever so slightly makeshift and unfinished.

ONE

SS2 People, performers, loads of others too: director, production manager, set designer, lighting designer, philosopher, experts and non-experts, seemingly random people, administrators, babies and baby sitters, choreographers, writers, interns and mentees etc. Performers that are people, people as performers, performers as people. More often than not, non-performers or non-professional performers at least, but not always, "performers" more or less playing versions of themselves, people "performing" themselves, or not performing at all perhaps, or only ever so slightly, but still somehow…

Quarantine's work dreams of a kind of raw directness of interaction and knowingly fails at this…full of issues, complicated issues and questions concerning life, death and politics. …a strange mix between the politics of representation and the representation of politics…flirting with failure, openly failing, but always staying stubborn…there is a lot of "empty fun" —fluffy animals, rabbit costumes, glitter curtains, star cloths, disco dancing, food and drink, soul and funk music, air guitar playing etc., etc., perhaps of course not so empty fun after all, the stuff of shared pleasure, pleasure of being alive and on display, pleasure of being alive and witnessing, touching, sharing this pleasure…

DP There's always chairs. Functional chairs. And very good soundtracks.

AL …Well, it has something to do with quality of presence… Quarantine manages to show us great performances by cherishing what is there already…

They make work that matters with people who are not seen on stage that much, people whom the media-driven society often marginalises. So ultimately what makes a Quarantine piece stand out from the rest is how deeply political it is.

AK …I'd say that a Quarantine piece becomes a Quarantine piece through the distinctiveness of its thinking — as theatre — and realisation of a necessary theatre-form. What form does that take? It depends on the thought. In other words, the aesthetic is not the end but the means for a processual logic of theatre-thinking.

GH …From what I've seen and felt I'd say a certain "thoughtfulness," although perhaps I mean "mindfulness." I get a strong sense that the shows are the product of a serious and respectful commitment to their subjects.

…The shows make a time/space that demands we simply pay careful attention to the performers and what they are doing and saying and where we, the audience are paid careful attention in return. Shouldn't all theatre and performance be like that? Well it's not.

TWO

EG ...the importance of our individual stories...of all the normal people who live life so fully but are rarely validated by representation in our cultural endeavours. In dance and performance it is still rare, I would say.

AK ...Questions about the nature of theatrical encounter, the relationship between stage and audience; questions about the nature of performing, about being-on-stage and beings-on-stage; questions, in other words, about specifically theatrical forms of ontology, about being-there and being-there-together; questions about appearance, reality, the pleasures of illusion; questions about the nature of the theatre as an environment, as a world in which certain things happen, and can be made to happen; questions about story—the stories we tell ourselves, the stories we live by; questions of relationality, about ourselves constructed through, and in relation to, others and the manifestation of these relations in traces of encounter, event and experience.

HB Identity. What is it that makes us who we are? What brings us together and what splits us apart?

THREE

MF The taste of a single cherry in Leicester.

SS2 Memories remain. Questions remain too: like why do it like that? Why is it not working? And yet why is it nevertheless? A sense of a genuine encounter with the performers that was extremely pleasurable but not necessarily "easy." If we as audience are paid attention to we are not "pandered to."

Three generic things:Set design—simple, beautiful.
Sense of community—being part of the gathering for that

show/event. The bravery of people to tell their stories with such honesty.

LE It sticks around because when you go back to living, after a show, you suddenly see the art (and by art I mean thoughts, feelings, ideas) in your life, your everyday existence. I feel a bit illuminated. I feel a bit more sensitive to life.

FOUR

EG I am not so interested in grouping artists' work together. One of several key things I look for when programming is distinctiveness. What's interesting is the strength of an approach, and then the ideas and vocabulary employed within that approach.

FM The more we lost trust in the reality around us, the more we learned that what you see is not what you get, the more obviously also our belief in representation of reality got awkward. And theatre—as THE medium of representation—seemed quite helpless in dealing with these new circumstances. The more we could not get a hold of reality anymore, the more the need for reality grew. Television invented **BIG BROTHER** and reality documentaries and fiction that looked like documentaries. And theatre started to think of short cuts, skipping representation (well, at least pretending to) and putting more real things directly on stage. Performers, dilettantes, etc replaced actors, Baktruppen from Norway swallowed sleeping pills and ended their performance snoring. Schlingensief brought disabled and ill people on stage, Needcompany filled the room with the smell of real cooking etc etc. Around 2000, "the real people" arrived on stage: Quarantine is one of the few that found its own way, its own aesthetics, its own technique and dramaturgy. It is not about who was first, it is—as always in art—about who finds a unique and adequate and radical way of working and making.

MF I remember early discussions with the company about a desire to create situations, facilitate un-plannable meetings of minds, and if the cast were to leave the room/stage/maze/party, no-one would notice and the event might carry on regardless, under its own steam. I see the same desire, differently expressed, in Lone Twin's GHOST DANCE and GOB SQUAD'S KITCHEN.

AK There is perhaps a certain family resemblance with other contemporary theatre-makers on the basis of the approach rather than the style or aesthetic: Rimini Protokoll (working with "experts of the everyday" alongside theatre professionals, utilising their expertise and facilitating "untrained" performances rather than over-coded "acting"); Victoria (working with young people, using their materials, concerns, ideas to make theatre at the cutting edge rather than as community "expression"); New York City Players (a commitment to story, to theatre-writing—and an apparently anti-theatrical but highly theatricalised aesthetic)…

AL What makes a Quarantine piece distinctive is the lack of anxiety on stage. They are not overtly occupied with trying to please their audiences. They simply ask them to witness the work. Those companies who know and respect the form understand its robustness and are able to interrogate it in their endeavour to throw new light on the world they see. Those companies such as Forced Entertainment, Lone Twin and Quarantine are pushing the form forward. They make very different work but they are united by a creative imperative—they make the work they have to make because it matters…

FIVE

SB/RG/RS Question removed

SIX

MT As an audience member I trust Quarantine to take me on a journey—it may be challenging or moving en route but it usually is surprisingly comforting in the end. Strangely, it makes you want to be one of the performers.

SH As a performer in ENTITLED I feel as if I have no edges, as if I am completely permeable and vulnerable even if I don't show it, I try not to. You have to trust Quarantine, and then you have to trust the audience, that they can't be fooled. You have to live with your failures. Having been the writer on work where I ask people to be themselves I've never understood before how much I've been asking of them.

DP It can be frustrating—you want to be comfortable but there are constant changes, the process never ends…But it's the nature of the work and contributes to the fragility of it. It's down to trust in the end. Nothing in a Quarantine show takes the piss or doesn't have a serious intent.

AK I think I look at the mechanism of their appearing—the relationship between the self-presentation and the "technique" of the theatrical apparatus, often virtuosic in its visible invisibility—rather than think about "just being yourself".

SS1 I've secretly always wanted to be in one!

SEVEN

SS2 …boundaries between the private and the public, when it comes to the revelation of the personal content, from the mundane to the traumatic. There is always a right to silence and to veto whether something personal is revealed in rehearsal or, if it has been, whether it makes it into a show.

Make-believe — Photo: Simon Banham

...There is clearly an "ethical" tension at play here, but one that is also productive, awkwardly interesting.

CT It usually seems (or are we led to believe) that performers are being open, honest, raw etc. This is especially so in their more vulnerable moments. However, is it as honest as is presented or do we just feel like it is?

AK Loads — mainly about agency and authorship, about the actor's awareness of the scene in which they are staged and "stage", but also about the spectator's capacity to co-compose the work with the performer/makers, to be invested in the creative process.

GH For me Quarantine's shows suspend easy judgments in relation to the performers and the material presented and allow for an "equality of intelligences" between all concerned. If forced to use the term — I'd call that "ethical."

FE I think that's an issue to be raised by performers who have participated in Quarantine's work, not by academics and critics in the sector. I find the whole conversation really distasteful, to imply that the performers aren't somehow capable of recognising whether they've being taken advantage of.

DP I chose and my mum chose to do everything we do. I'm too intelligent to be exploited by a theatre company. Class and economics define how we are viewed. We are proud of living in a council house in Manchester and we tour the world. It's not even an issue for me...

EIGHT

AK There's a lot resting on this, for me, that goes beyond any instrumentalist conception of "relational aesthetics." I'd say there's an awareness of the audience as co-creators

Make-believe — Photo: Simon Banham

of the theatre event, but a limit to the extent that such a knowledge determines the nature of the aesthetic itself. The spectator's work is acknowledged without being pre-determined — where it is, the work seems to over-assert itself. I sometimes think this about the "banquet" or meal set-up of some of the works — we know we participate (as spectators) already, does this really need to be re-asserted? Does our capacity to relate become reduced by the explication of relationality itself? Depends, I guess…

LE I think it's about the feeling you create, like we're all in on it. The audience, the performers. Those definitions feel incidental a lot of the time. All the space you leave for audience thought and interaction and contribution make each show unknown until it's happened.

Also, by acknowledging the audience, maybe that's what gives me so much to think about after, I can't ignore it, I've been active and engaged with people and ideas.

MF There's a text by Walter Benjamin on Brecht that seems relevant, if only tangentially.

"The moment when the mass begins to differentiate itself in discussion and responsible decisions, or in attempts to discover well-founded attitudes of its own, the moment the false and deceptive totality called "audience" begins to disintegrate and there is space for the formation of separate parties within it — separate parties corresponding to conditions as they really are — at that moment the critic suffers the double misfortune of seeing his nature as agent revealed and, at the same time, devalued." In other words, for me all Quarantine shows are for an audience of one, in a genuine and lived engagement (and sometimes actual discussion) with performers, and sometimes with other audiences of one.

NINE

SS2 …it alienates audiences through its intimacy, through its ethical risk taking, its inevitable failure for everyone to feel comfortable at sharing this information.

…but, cutting across all these different types of alienation, the work is able to find a lot of fans…

LD I would argue that your work also connects audiences that wouldn't ordinarily collide!

SH …Possibly an audience member has to have been previously amazed and delighted by the smallest of things or the strange emotional jolt which is caused by two oppositional things being brought together to appreciate those moments when they appear in a Quarantine show.

MF …there's a camp that wants the grit, the conflict, the desire somehow made manifest onstage; engaged with or presented theatrically. And for them, work that doesn't do this, however well conceived or performed or structured, seems apolitical, or irrelevant; or at least just not theatre. For plenty of us though, a politics, and a sadness at why things are not, you know, different, is pretty clear in the work.

EG I imagine the reason why the work polarises people is that it is not focussed on the transformative. This is not to say you will not be taken off to new places during a show, but that they work by gentle persuasion, not by trickery. Some people may miss the mastery of presenting the normal.

TEN

GH I'm disappointed that because the shows depend on particular performers, most cannot be "revived". I would so like to have seen **WHITE TRASH**...I have a feeling that this was quite an "important" show...**OLD PEOPLE, CHILDREN AND ANIMALS** (Devised in 2008 with five performers over 65, a teenage-girl rock band, two toddlers, seven white rabbits and a parrot). The "old people" didn't seem that old to me. But also I felt that you might have not asked the older women the right sort of questions and/or didn't manage to create a situation in which they really "owned" the material.

SS2 ...latent frustrations, curbed desires, second thoughts, general uncertainty, and pleasure from being able to just leave it be. I have never been disappointed from seeing a Quarantine show, even when I thought there was a lot wrong with it, I have always thoroughly enjoyed it on many levels. This is a rare phenomenon.

MF ...in very specific ways that, perhaps through a making process that in the end just didn't quite gel, or a repetition (the result of success) that begins to see spontaneity of thought performed rather than a space created for thought, for emotion. But these are also the reasons I will keep coming back—as their true presence, thought and emotion, are always a real possibility, and from quite mundane and everyday source material. If there is transcendence, it has to be earned, and it will be fleeting. You might have just missed it.

ELEVEN

MB ...What is challenging about working with Quarantine is precisely what is pleasurable: namely, the fact that the discussion of philosophical ideas is directly informed by, and seeks to be directly relevant to, the lives of the performers and the people making the show. There is thus a point of contact between philosophical ideas and the lives and histories of those involved in the production that makes discussion more difficult, more serious and yet more relevant, than much of the philosophical discussions that take place in the lecture theatre or seminar room.

SS2 There is, of course, the pleasure of the challenge itself. The challenge lies perhaps most of all in the intensity of communication across differences, in the negotiation of interactions with the many members of the rehearsal process.

LE For me, a challenge is afterwards, you can't look at anything in the same way again! And then I understand. All the work that goes into a Quarantine piece of work isn't just the examination of things, but the selection of things, and it's a very fine craft.

SH The pleasure in terms of writing is that I very rarely have to make anything up. I have to chat and listen to the people who are in the show, and they tell me about themselves, and we find out things that we have in common, and I ask cheekier questions as I get to know them and they answer them or not — either is interesting — and if they don't answer, then I ask them why not, and then usually the "why not" answer becomes the thing that they say. I like writing a Quarantine show, because my job is really as an editor of text — it has to be about the craft of writing, finding the clearest, simplest, most uncluttered way of saying something quite complex. And then the smallest of words, especially the conjunctives become really interesting. The challenge in this way of working is how to give back the person's story using their words in something close to their way of speaking but with my questions, my concerns concealed within what they have said. The trick is to render yourself invisible.

TWELVE

MT Like a man who unexpectedly stands up to tell his life story on a crowded bus.

FE Like the last half an hour of a high school disco, the very moment before the lights all come back on and it's just a gymnasium again.

Quarantine's work has a visual aesthetic as beautiful and convincing as the work itself. There is often a simple ordinariness about the design, an apparent casualness as if they have just used what is to hand. The concept and the design are inextricable.

AL That slow, slow fade in GRACE remains with me and is still astonishing every time I recall it.

MF Like walking down the street: mundane in long-shot, fascinating close-up.

LD Brutal honesty, beautifully presented.

SS1 Like LIFE.

THIRTEEN

This one is for you…

THE QUESTIONS

1. What is it that makes a Quarantine piece a Quarantine piece?
2. Are there any questions that you see recurring in Quarantine's work?
3. What remains for you, from any experience of a Quarantine piece?
4. Where does Quarantine's work sit in relation to other contemporary performance?
5. We've recently started saying that our work is about "the here and now." What do you think about that?
6. What is it like to see (or be) a performer in a Quarantine

piece, working with their (your) own history as a source for material?
7. Are there any ethical issues that arise for you when you think about what Quarantine does?
8. We talk a lot about relationships with audience when we make our work. Are there ways that we engage with audiences that you've noticed are a particularly "Quarantine" way of working?
9. Our work often divides or polarises audiences. Any ideas why?
10. In what ways do we disappoint you?
11. Are there particular challenges or pleasures involved in helping us to develop our work? What are they?
12. What does Quarantine's work look like?
13. Are there any other questions we should have asked?

AUTHOR BIOGRAPHIES

NO MORE DRAMA

AUTHOR BIOGRAPHIES

CHRISTIANE KÜHL is a Berlin based journalist and theatre maker. She worked as arts editor for the daily newspaper Taz, Die Tageszeitung (Berlin), the monthly magazine Kultur Spiegel (Hamburg) and as news editor for public radio Radio Eins (Berlin). In 2004 she began freelancing for print and audio, and also to work as author/dramaturg/performer with video designer and director Chris Kondek. Together they have made seven performances, including the internationally-acclaimed stock market play **DEAD CAT BOUNCE** (co-produced with Rotterdamse Schouwburg), **MONEY — IT CAME FROM OUTER SPACE** (co-produced with Hebbel am Ufer Berlin) and, most recently, the fake documentary **EVEN THE DEAD ARE NOT SAFE FROM THE LIVING** (Mousonturm Frankfurt). Starting from 2012 she will join the artistic direction panel of the Berliner Festspiele.

CECILIA SOSA is an Argentinean sociologist, cultural journalist, and PhD candidate in Drama at Queen Mary, University of London. She moved to the UK in 2007 with a British Council award to undertake an MA in Critical and Creative Writing at Goldsmiths, which she finished in 2008 with distinction. Since then, her performance research to explore the new connections and affects that emerged in the aftermath of Argentina's last dictatorship (1974–1983). She published "On Mothers and Spiders: A face-to-face encounter with Argentina's mourning" in *Memory Studies*, and "A Counter-narrative of Argentine Mourning: The Headless Woman (2008), directed by Lucrecia Martel" in *Theory, Culture & Society* and *'Beau Travail (1998) and Judith Butler*. Dancing at the limits of Queer Melancholia' in *Cultural Studies*. She has also written reviews for E-misférica New Theatre Quarterly, and Contemporary Theatre Review, and is one of the contributors to Memory of State Terrorism in the Southern Cone (Palgrave Macmillan, 2011), where she proposes a provocative reading of the Mothers of Plaza de Mayo's performance alongside the Argentine film *Los rubios* (2003), by Albertina Carri.

JACOB WREN is a writer and maker of eccentric performances. His books include *Unrehearsed Beauty*, *Families Are Formed Through Copulation* and *Revenge Fantasies of the Politically Dispossessed*. These books have been translated into French and published by Le Quartanier. As co-artistic director of Montreal-based interdisciplinary group PME-ART he has co-created **EN FRANCAIS COMME EN ANGLAIS, IT'S EASY TO CRITICIZE** (1998), **UNREHEARSED BEAUTY (LE GÉNIE DES AUTRES,** 2002), **LA FAMILLE SE CRÉE EN COPULANT** (2005) and the ongoing **HOSPITALITÉ (HOSPITALITY)** series which includes: 1: **THE TITLE IS CONSTANTLY CHANGING** (2007), 2: **GRADUALLY THIS OVERVIEW** (2010), 3: **INDIVIDUALISM WAS A MISTAKE** (2008) and 5: **THE DJ WHO GAVE TOO MUCH INFORMATION** (2011).

AUTHOR BIOGRAPHIES

He has also collaborated with Nadia Ross and her company STO Union. Together they have co-written and co-directed **RECENT EXPERIENCES** (2000) and **REVOLUTIONS IN THERAPY** (2004). In 2007 he was invited by Sophiensaele (Berlin) to adapt and direct Wolfgang Koeppen's 1954 novel *Der Tod in Rom* and in 2008 he was commissioned by Campo (Ghent) to collaborate with Pieter De Buysser on **AN ANTHOLOGY OF OPTIMISM**. He frequently writes about contemporary art.

DENISE LUCCIONI was born in French Algeria, and grew up in Turkey, England, and Germany. After receiving an MA in American literature, she reoriented her life after encountering Trisha Brown, Steve Paxton and John Cage in the mid-1970s. In Paris, she worked with Benedicte Pesle (Merce Cunningham and Bob Wilson's representative since the 1960s) became Richard Foreman's assistant in Paris and New York, co-founded the Cinémathèque de la danse, co-directed the Théâtre de la Bastille in Paris, curated the new Paris American Centre in Performing Arts and Literature and the first events of **"L'ESPRIT DU NOMADE"** at the Cartier Foundation in Paris. She has acted as "artistic liaison" for international projects such as Act French in New York, in the mid 2000s. She has also translated books and DVDs (on Cunningham, Paxton and Halprin) and for theatre productions (including Foreman, Laurie Anderson, Robert Ashley, Richard Maxwell, Big Art Group, The Wooster Group). Neither a journalist, nor an academic, nor a historian, she writes and lectures about the artforms she knows best and is currently filming a series of experimental essays (homemade portraits of artists).

FLORIAN MALZACHER is co-curator of the interdisciplinary steirischer herbst festival in Graz/Austria (since 2006) and since 2009 also freelance dramaturg/curator for Burgtheater Vienna. After graduating in Applied Theatre Studies at the University of Giessen/Germany, he worked as a freelance theatre journalist for major daily papers and magazines. He is a founding member of the independent curators' collective, Unfriendly Takeover, in Frankfurt. He has worked as a freelance dramaturg (for Rimini Protokoll, Lola Arias & Stefan Kaegi, Nature Theater of Oklahoma) and has taught at the Universities of Vienna and Frankfurt, among others. He is member of the advisory board of Das Arts — Master of Theatre, Amsterdam, as well as advisor for Schillertage at Nationaltheater Mannheim. Florian regularly writes about contemporary theatre and dance, and has co-written and co-edited several books, including *Not Even a Game Anymore — The Theatre of Forced Entertainment* (2004), *Experts of the Everyday — The Theatre of Rimini Protokoll* (2008), and *Frakcija #55 on Curating Performing Arts* (2010, together with Tea Tupajic and Petra Zanki).

AUTHOR BIOGRAPHIES

NOELIA RUIZ is a PhD Researcher in the Drama Studies Centre in University College Dublin, investigating Contemporary Theatre and Performance Creative Processes with a focus on Irish companies. She belongs to IFTR's Working Group Creative Processes: Genetics of Performance convened by Josette Féral, and TAPRA working group Directing & Dramaturgy. She holds a MA in Directing for Theatre (UCD, 2007) and also holds several qualifications in performance arts from Trinity Guildhall London. Noelia has trained with artists such as Anne Bogart SITI Company, Lisa Nelson, Oscar McLennan, Anne Seagrave, Matteo Destro, Quarantine Theatre Company, Caroline McSweeney and Ruth Zaporah. In March, 2010 she was awarded an artistic residency in MAKE, a residential laboratory in Ireland. In June, 2010 she was also part of Project Brand New Generation. In 2010, she directed the interactive multilingual theatre piece **THE CAPPUCCINO CULTURE** in the ABSOLUT Fringe Festival to sold out houses. In 2011 she presented **BETTER LOVED FROM AFAR**, which explored the relationship between photography, narrative and performance in documentary form around the subject of the Irish Diaspora in Argentina.

FRANCISCO FRAZÃO was born in Lisbon in 1978. He graduated in Modern Languages and Literatures (Portuguese and English) at the University of Lisbon and should be working on his PhD in Comparative Studies. He collaborated with theatre company Artistas Unidos from 2000 to 2004, working as translator, dramaturg and editor of the company's magazine. Since 2004 he is the theatre programmer at Culturgest. Francisco has translated works by Beckett, Pinter, Stephen Greenhorn, Howard Barker, Tim Crouch, Abi Morgan, Katori Hall and Chris Thorpe. He has written for newspapers and magazines on theatre, film and literature.

CHANTAL HURAULT has a PhD in Theatre Studies, teaches at the Sorbonne Nouvelle (Paris) and also works for the City Theatre, the Festival d'Avignon and currently the Comédie- Française. She is a member of the Editorial Board of Alternatives Théâtrales.

SARAH GORMAN is Principal Lecturer in Drama, Theatre & Performance Studies at Roehampton University, London. Her research explores feminist performance and contemporary European and North American experimental theatre. Her book *The Theatre of Richard Maxwell and the New York City Players* was published by Routledge in May, 2011. She has contributed to *Making Contemporary Theatre: International Rehearsal Processes* (edited Jen Harvie & Andy Lavender, 2010); *Performance and the Contemporary City* (edited by Nicolas Whybrow, 2010); *Bobby Baker: Redeeming Features of Daily Life* (edited by Bobby Baker and Michèle Barrett, 2007) and *A Concise Companion to British and Irish*

AUTHOR BIOGRAPHIES

Drama (edited Nadine Holdsworth and Mary Luckhurst, 2008).

SODJA ZUPANC LOTKER is Artistic Director of the Prague Quadrennial of Performance Design and Space. She has worked for this scenography event since 1999. She also works as a dramaturg for independent theatre, dance and site specific projects in Czech Republic, USA, Brazil etc., for instance with CIA Dani Lima, Farm in the Cave as well as Lhotakova/Soukup dance company. She has been teaching and giving lectures at Visual Arts Academy in Brno, Prague Performing Arts Academy, Columbia University, and a number of festivals and symposia. And is a PhD candidate in theatre theory at Vienna University.

ARTISTS SIMON BANHAM, RICHARD GREGORY AND RENNY O'SHEA set up Quarantine in 1998. They make theatre and other public events. Past projects have included family parties, radio broadcasts and journeys in the dark for one person at a time—as well as performances on stage for audiences in seats.

PETER CRAWLEY is a journalist and critic. He has been writing for The Irish Times since 2000 and has been the paper's chief theatre critic since 2007. He writes features and "Stage Struck," a column on theatre. Since 2002, he been News Editor of Irish Theatre Magazine and served as the magazine's Online Editor from 2003 to 2009. From 2009 to 2010 he taught "Contemporary Irish Theatre in Context" at Trinity College Dublin. He has contributed reviews and features to publications including The Sunday Times, The Sunday Business Post, The Dubliner, The Scotsman and Público, and broadcast on RTÉ Television, RTÉ Radio, Newstalk, BBC Radio Ulster and Phantom FM. He has a degree in Theatre Studies and English Literature from Trinity College Dublin and holds a masters in journalism from the Dublin Institute of Technology. He lives in Dublin.

WILLIE WHITE is Artistic Director of Dublin Theatre Festival. From 2002–2011 he was Artistic Director of Project Arts Centre, Dublin. Before that he worked for four years in RTÉ, Ireland's public service broadcaster, mostly on television arts programmes. Willie read for Master's degrees in English at University College Dublin and in Irish Theatre at Trinity College Dublin.

SUPPORT

NO MORE DRAMA

COLOPHON

EDITED BY PETER CRAWLEY & WILLIE WHITE

© THE WRITERS
PUBLISHED BY PROJECT PRESS, AN IMPRINT
OF PROJECT ARTS CENTRE, IN ASSOCIATION
WITH CARYSFORT PRESS

ISBN 978-1-872493-33-6

ALL RIGHTS RESERVED. NO PART OF THIS
PUBLICATION MAY BE REPRODUCED IN
WHOLE OR IN PART WITHOUT PRIOR
WRITTEN PERMISSION OF THE PUBLISHERS.
OOH, IT FEELS SO GOOD WHEN YOU LET GO
OF ALL THE DRAMA IN YOUR LIFE.

GRAPHIC LAYOUT BY R. WATKINS & J. CANELL
PROOFREADING: KATE HEFFERNAN
PRINTING: HUDSON KILLEEN LIMITED
EDITION: 750 COPIES

PROJECT ARTS CENTRE, 39 EAST ESSEX
STREET, TEMPLE BAR, DUBLIN 2, IRELAND
+353 1 881 9613
INFO@PROJECTARTSCENTRE.IE
WWW.PROJECTARTSCENTRE.IE

CARYSFORT PRESS, 58 WOODFIELD,
SCHOLARSTOWN ROAD, RATHFARNHAM,
DUBLIN 16, IRELAND
+353 1 493 7383
INFO@CARYSFORTPRESS.COM
WWW.CARYSFORTPRESS.COM

COVER IMAGE: PAN PAN THEATRE COMPANY,
PLAYBOY OF THE WESTERN WORLD

NO MORE DRAMA